THE TRIAL OF PAK TAL *AND OTHER STORIES*

THE TRIAL OF PAK TAL *AND OTHER STORIES*

Published in 2022 by Seoul Selection U.S.A., Inc.
4199 Campus Drive, Suite 550, Irvine, CA 92612
Phone: 949-509-6584 / Seoul office: 82-2-734-9567
Fax: 949-509-6599 / Seoul office: 82-2-734-9562
Email: hankinseoul@gmail.com
Website: www.seoulselection.com

ISBN: 978-1-62412-148-7
Printed in the Republic of Korea
The Work is published under the support of Literature Translation
Institute of Korea (LTI Korea).

THE TRIAL OF
PAK TAL *AND*
OTHER STORIES

Kim Tal-su

Translated with an Introduction by

Christopher D. Scott

Seoul Selection

Contents

Dedication

This translation is dedicated to the memory of my grandmother,
Katharine Sutherland O'Brien (1920–2014)—
or, as I knew her, Gramama.

Acknowledgments

I first encountered Kim Tal-su's work in graduate school at Stanford University in 1997, the same year that Kim passed away, so this translation has been a long time in the making. First, I would like to thank the Literature Translation Institute of Korea for selecting me to translate this work. I am also grateful to the staff at Seoul Selection for their help and patience during the editing and publication process. At Stanford, Tom Hare, Indra Levy, Jim Reichert, John Treat, and Atsuko Ueda were always encouraging of my work. During my research in Japan, which was funded by the IIE Fulbright Program and the Japan Foundation, Kanai Keiko, Kitagawa Taeko, Ko Youngran, Kōno Kensuke, Nakaya Izumi, and Park Yu-ha were kind and generous beyond compare. Special thanks to Levy Hideo for inspiring me in so many ways.

At Macalester College, Nadine Attewell, Frederik Green, Winston Kyan, Jim Laine, Peter Rachleff, and Satoko Suzuki were wonderful colleagues and mentors. Also, I would like to thank my amazing colleagues and students at The Nueva School, especially the following people: Diane Rosenberg for approving this project on top of my other duties, the students in my course "Fifty Words for Snow: Translation Studies" for their feedback on earlier drafts of this translation, my student Sasha Filippova for helping me with the Russian translation of "Paku Tari no saiban," and most of all my former student Brandon Cho for his meticulous research and editorial assistance. Last, but not least, I could not have finished this book without the love and support of my husband Weishiun Tsai, whom I also met in 1997 and who has been by my side ever since.

Acknowledgments

A Note on Names and Romanization

Names are a deeply personal and political issue for
Koreans in Japan due to the so-called "name-changing
campaign" (*sōshi kaimei*), which forced Koreans to adopt
Japanese (or Japanized) names during the colonial period,
and the immigration and naturalization policies of
postwar Japan, which often forced or encouraged Koreans
in Japan to hide their real names (*honmyō*) and use
assumed names (*tsūmei*).

Names also play an important role in Kim Tal-su's
literature, as these stories clearly demonstrate. Thus, I
have tried to render names as accurately and consistently
as possible. Kim often uses the ambiguity or double
valence between Japanese and Korean names to highlight
the multiple identities and dilemmas that Koreans face
when passing as Japanese or living in Japan. When

THE TRIAL OF PAK TAL AND OTHER STORIES

necessary, I have included the Chinese characters for names that have multiple readings or meanings in the text.

Throughout this translation, East Asian names are given in East Asian order (i.e., surname first). For romanization, I have followed the McCune-Reischauer system for Korean names, the modified Hepburn system for Japanese names, and the Hanyu Pinyin system for Chinese names, except in the case of personal and place names that have more common English spellings (e.g., Syngman Rhee, Park Chung-hee, Tokyo, and Seoul).

A Note on Names and Romanization

Translator's Introduction

Kim Tal-su (1920–1997) occupies a particularly prominent place in the history of Japanese-language literature by Koreans in Japan (so-called Zainichi Koreans). To begin with, he was one of the first Zainichi Koreans to write in Japanese, publishing his first story in 1940 at the age of twenty, while Korea was still a Japanese colony and Koreans were considered Japanese citizens—albeit second-class ones—and were encouraged to write in Japanese as a way of demonstrating their "Japaneseness." Second, he became one of the most prolific Zainichi Korean writers and intellectuals in postwar Japan, publishing more than sixty books in Japanese and more than fifty works of fiction, including many novels, novellas, and short stories. In 1980, he became the first living Zainichi Korean author to have his work reissued

THE TRIAL OF PAK TAL AND OTHER STORIES

in a collected works, which spanned seven volumes.[1] More recently, his work was included in the first volume of the *"Zainichi" bungaku zenshū* (Collected works of "Zainichi" literature), the first anthology of Zainichi Korean literature.[2] Finally, there has been a resurgence of interest in his life and work since his death in 1997, including a number of academic studies in Japanese, a 2014 paperback collection of his work (on which this translation is based), and a special exhibition on him at the Kanagawa Museum of Modern Literature in 2021, in honor of the 100th anniversary of his birth.[3]

As these examples suggest, Kim was a giant in the

---

1 Kimu Darusu, *Kimu Darusu shōsetsu zenshū*, 7 vols. (Tokyo: Chikuma Shobō, 1980).

2 Isogai Jirō and Kuroko Kazuo, eds., *"Zainichi" bungaku zenshū*, Vol. 1 (Tokyo: Bensei Shuppan, 2006).

3 Recent monographs on Kim include: Choi Hyoson, *Kaikyō ni tatsu hito: Kimu Darusu no bungaku to shōgai* (Tokyo: Hihyōsha, 1998); Shin Gi-su, *Kimu Darusu runesansu: bungaku · rekishi · minzoku* (Tokyo: Kaihō Shuppansha, 2002); Hirose Yōichi, *Kimu Darusu to sono jidai: bungaku · kodaishi · kokka* (Tokyo: Crane, 2016); and Hirose Yōichi, *Nihon no naka no Chōsen: Kimu Darusu den* (Tokyo: Crane, 2019). This translation is based on the texts in Kimu Darusu, *Kimu Darusu shōsetsu shū* (Tokyo: Kōdansha, 2014), with the exception of "Fuji no mieru mura de," which has already been translated into English.

field of Zainichi Korean literature, not to mention
Japanese literature. Japanese sociologist Tsurumi
Shunsuke jokingly called him "King" Tal-su, playing off a
Japanese reading of Kim's surname (Kin), while Japanese
historian Ueda Masaaki dubbed him "Donarudo Kin," a
multilingual pun on both Donald Keene, the pioneering
American scholar and translator of Japanese literature,
and Kim's legendary short temper (the Japanese word
donaru means "to shout").[4] Despite Kim's prodigious
literary output and foundational role in the formation
of the genre now known as Zainichi Korean literature,
there are still relatively few studies of him in English
and even fewer English translations of his work.[5] This

_____

4 Tsurumi Shunsuke, "Kimu Darusu: sokoku bundan to sabetsu kara
   umareta Nihongo bungaku," *Ushio* (April 2001): 291. Ueda Masaaki once
   quipped, "Sarcastic people would call Kim Tal-su the Donald Kin of
   zainichi Koreans, likening him to Donald Keene, the American literary
   scholar. [Kim] had the tendency to fly off the handle, screaming [*donaru*]
   in public. [. . .] That's how he got the nickname Donald 'Loudmouth' Kin
   [*Donarudo Kin*]. [Kim] cut quite a figure, with his large frame and loud
   voice." Quoted in Shin (2002, 102–103).

5 English-language studies of Kim's work include: Christopher D. Scott,
   "Invisible Men: The *Zainichi* Korean Presence in Postwar Japanese
   Culture," doctoral dissertation (Stanford University, 2006), especially
   Chapter 1; Jonathan Glade, "Failed Solidarity: Confronting Imperial
   Structures in Kim Sa-ryang's 'Into the Light' and Kim Tal-su's 'Village

translation aims to bring greater attention to Kim's work, both as literary texts in their own right and as artifacts of Zainichi Korean cultural production. Why was Kim such an important and respected writer? What do his works tell us about the Zainichi Korean experience in modern Japan? And how did his writing evolve over time in response to changing historical and political conditions? This brief introduction will attempt to answer these questions by providing an overview of Kim's life and career, particularly in relation to the works translated in this collection, and by considering the larger significance of his writing, both for understanding the development of Zainichi Korean identity and for thinking about Japan, Korea, and Japanese-Korean relations in new ways.

---

with a View of Mt. Fuji,'" *Sungkyun Journal of East Asian Studies* 17(2) (October 2017): 191–210; Christina Yi, *Colonizing Language: Cultural Production and Language Politics in Modern Japan and Korea* (New York: Columbia University Press, 2018), especially Chapter 5; and Robert J. Del Greco, "Democratic Empire: Expatriate Koreans in Japan Write Against Empire," doctoral dissertation (Ohio State University, 2018). English translations of Kim's work include: Kim Tal-su, "In the Shadow of Mt. Fuji," trans. Sharalyn Orbaugh, in *Into the Light: An Anthology of Literature by Koreans in Japan*, ed. Melissa L. Wender (Honolulu: University of Hawai'i Press, 2010), 39–65; and Kim Talsu, "Trash," trans. Christina Yi, in *Zainichi Literature: Japanese Writings by Ethnic Koreans*, ed. John Lie (Berkeley: Institute of East Asian Studies, 2018), 35–53.

Translator's Introduction

Kim Tal-su was born on January 17, 1920, in a small
village in Gyeongsangnam-do near present-day Masan
in Changwon, South Korea.[6] Like many Koreans during
the colonial period (1910–1945), the family fell on hard
times, forcing Kim's father to take his mother and two of
his siblings to Japan in 1925 in search of a better life. Kim
stayed behind in Korea with his grandmother and his
older brother, who died three years later, followed by his
father. In 1930, at the age of ten, Kim moved to Japan to
join his remaining family members. He writes movingly
of these experiences, especially his fond memories of his
grandmother, in "Sobo no omoide," translated here as
"Memories of My Grandmother." Kim first published
this text in 1944 in the coterie journal *Keirin* (Kyerim, an
ancient name for Korea). After the war, he republished it
under the penname Son In-jang in the April 1946 issue
of the leftist journal *Minshu Chōsen* (Democratic Korea).
Although it seems fairly straightforward, this story is
more complicated than it appears. By memorializing
his late grandmother, who insisted on being buried in
her ancestral home of Korea, and reminiscing about his

6 For a detailed biography of Kim Tal-su's life and career, see: Hirose, *Kimu
Darusu to sono jidai*, 422–448.

hometown, Kim was sending a subtle yet unmistakable message about his ethnic identity at a time when being Korean—or, more precisely, being proud of being Korean—was at odds with the late colonial project of assimilating Koreans as Japanese and eradicating Korean culture. Moreover, by the time he republished the text in 1946, Koreans in Japan had become stateless subjects with no clear or easy way to return to their homeland. In other words, "Memories of My Grandmother" is not just a Proustian remembrance of the past; it is a powerful political statement about being uprooted or displaced and trying to find one's way home, both literally and figuratively.

After moving to Tokyo in 1930, Kim lived the rest of his life mostly in Japan, but he never felt fully at home there, no doubt because he was so conscious and proud of his Korean ethnic identity. He began learning Japanese by attending elementary school in Japan and working various odd jobs, such as selling *nattō* (fermented soybeans) and collecting trash, to help his family make ends meet. In the trash, he found Japanese magazines such as *Shōnen kurabu* (Boys' Club) and books such as *Gendai Nihon bungaku zenshū* (Collected works of contemporary Japanese literature), which he read voraciously. Many Koreans worked as trash collectors and were often treated like garbage in Japan, so it is perhaps not surprising that Kim first found his own voice in Japanese by reading books and magazines thrown away in the trash. He was particularly fond of the Japanese Naturalist writer Shiga Naoya, whose semi-autobiographical style left a deep impression on him. Indeed, Kim's debut work, "Ichi," translated here as "One's Place," is loosely based on his own experience living with a Japanese roommate during college. Kim published "One's Place" under the penname Ōsawa Tatsuo in the August 1940 issue of *Geijutsuka* (College of Art), a literary magazine produced by the Nihon University College of Art, where Kim enrolled in 1939. This story was inspired by another story by a Korean writer: Kim Sa-ryang's "Hikari no naka ni" (Into the light, 1939), which was nominated for the prestigious Akutagawa Prize in 1940.[7]

---

7 Kimu Saryan, "Hikari no naka ni," *Hikari no naka ni: Kimu Saryan sakuhin shū* (Tokyo: Kōdansha, 1999), 10–56. For an English translation of "Hikari no naka ni," see: Kim Sa-ryang, "Into the Light," trans. Christopher D. Scott, in *Into the Light: An Anthology of Literature by Koreans in Japan*, ed. Melissa L. Wender (Honolulu: University of Hawai'i Press, 2010), 13–38. For an analysis of "Hikari no naka ni," see: Nayoung

Unlike the more assimilationist and pro-Japanese (or at least pretending-to-be-Japanese) tone of "Hikari no naka ni," "One's Place" is much more skeptical and critical of the colonial ideology of "Japan and Korea as one body" (*naisen ittai*), which was dominant at the time. In this story, the Korean narrator Chang Ŭng-sŏ, who goes by the Japanese name Ōsawa Teruo, has a falling out with his racist Japanese roommate Tanaami Kisaku, who himself is passing as someone he is not. In the final scene, Tanaami reminds Chang/Ōsawa of his place or position (*ichi*) as a Korean in Japanese society, causing Chang/Ōsawa to move out, presumably to find a place of his own. Thus, while the story problematizes Japanese racism and discrimination toward Koreans as well as the social and emotional costs of passing, it also envisions a "room of one's own," so to speak, for Koreans in Japan, much like "Hikari no naka ni" does.

After 1945, when Japan lost the war and its empire, the situation for Koreans in Japan changed dramatically. Many of them were now stranded in Japan, unable or

---

Aimee Kwon, *Intimate Empire: Collaboration and Colonial Modernity in Korea and Japan* (Durham and London: Duke University Press, 2015), especially Chapters 3 and 4.

Translator's Introduction

unwilling to go back to Korea, which soon descended into civil war, and were faced with the daunting prospect of living as former colonial subjects in a country that no longer wanted them there. During the hardscrabble years of the Occupation period (1945–1952), many Koreans in postwar Japan were forced to eke out a living by engaging in illicit or illegal activities, such as brewing *t'akchu* (a kind of moonshine), selling candy, or collecting scrap metal. Kim had spent much of the war moving back and forth between Japan and Korea, working for newspapers based in Yokohama and Keijō (Seoul), but after August 15, 1945, he settled down in Yokosuka and quickly became involved in Zainichi Korean leftist political organizations such as the League of Koreans in Japan (Chōren for short) and leftist Japanese literary groups such as the New Japanese Literature Association (Shin Nihon Bungakkai). This is when he began his literary career in earnest, co-founding the journal *Minshu Chōsen* (Democratic Korea), where he published many of his earliest works, such as *Kōei no machi* (City of Descendants, 1946–1947). During this period of intense productivity, he published "Takuju no kanpai," translated here as "Kindred Spirits" but which might also be translated as "A Toast with *T'akchu*," in

THE TRIAL OF PAK TAL AND OTHER STORIES

the September 1948 issue of the Japanese journal *Shichō* (Current Thought). Set during the final months of the war, this story focuses on the relationship between An Tong-sun (Andō Jun), a Korean reporter for a local newspaper who passes as Japanese but tries to help his fellow Koreans, and Kōyama (Hwang) Ungi, a Korean who works for the Japanese secret police and spies on Koreans suspected of bootlegging. In the final scene, An/Andō takes Kōyama/Hwang out for drinks in a Korean slum, forcing him to drink *t'akchu* and eat *ttongch'ang* (offal) as a way of proving who is more Korean. The "kindred spirits" of the title refers to both the similarity between Korean *t'akchu* and Japanese *doburoku*, which are written with the same Chinese character (濁酒) and which were extremely popular at the time, but also the kinship and bad blood between An/Andō and Kōyama/Hwang, which form the core of the story. In addition to its vivid portrayal of the lives of ordinary Koreans on the fringes of Japanese society, this story exposes the fine line between assimilation and resistance—or between obeying the law and breaking it—for Zainichi Koreans in postwar Japan.

During the 1950s, the Zainichi Korean community became more and more fractured, largely due to the

Korean War (1950–1953) and political infighting among Zainichi Korean organizations, which split the community along political and ideological lines. Kim's writing also became more bifurcated, as shown by the alternating perspectives of his magnum opus *Genkai nada* (The Genkai Sea, 1952–1953). By the late 1950s, he found himself ostracized from both the North Korea-aligned General Association of Korean Residents in Japan (Chongryon for short) and the Japanese Communist Party.[8] Moreover, he had reached an impasse in his writing. He was struggling to find a new "approach" (*shiten*) to fiction.[9] He found it in the 1958 novella "Paku Tari no saiban," translated here as "The Trial of Pak Tal," which is one of his most highly acclaimed works. In 1959, it was nominated for the prestigious Akutagawa Prize,

---

8 For more information about Kim's split with these groups, see: Ko Youngran, "The Korean War and Disputed Memories: Kim Dal-su's *Nihon no fuyu* and the 1955 System," trans. Michael K. Bourdaghs, in *Literature among the Ruins, 1945–1955*, eds. Atsuko Ueda, Michael K. Bourdaghs, Richi Sakakibara, and Hirokazu Toeda (Lanham, MD: Lexington Books, 2018), 43–59. Also see: Ko Youngran, "*Sengo" to iu ideorogii: rekishi/kioku/bunka* (Tokyo: Fujiwara Shoten, 2010), especially Chapters 6 and 7.

9 Hirose, *Kimu Darusu to sono jidai*, 122–126 and 143–147.

usually given to new writers, but Kim was disqualified for being a veteran writer. Nonetheless, the Japanese judges were effusive in their praise. The eminent Japanese writer Kawabata Yasunari described it as "a work of a different caliber" (*kaku no chigau sakuhin*) than the other nominees.[10] During the early 1960s, it was adapted into a play and performed around the country. In 1967, it was translated into Russian, probably because of its socialist message and its references to Nikolai Gogol's 1842 novel *Dead Souls*.[11] "The Trial of Pak Tal" is a humorous yet serious tale about a South Korean farmhand named Pak Tal who undergoes a political awakening during the Korean War and becomes a leftist revolutionary who eventually organizes a labor strike at an American military base for which he is brought to trial. There are many ways to read this revolutionary work: as a political satire, as a protest novel, or even as a critique of the Japanese discourse of *tenkō* (ideological conversion), as

---

10 Kawabata Yasunari, "Sayoku bungaku no kasaku," *Bungei Shunjū* (March 1953): 289.

11 Kin Tatsu Dzyu, *Sud Nad Pak Talem*, trans. V. Logunovoy (Moscow: Progress, 1967).

Hirose Yōichi has argued.[12] Here, I would like to suggest another way to read it: as an allegory of Zainichi Korean subjectivity and subterfuge. Indeed, the narrative is split between the chatty and unreliable narrator, whose true identity remains a mystery, and Pak Tal, who is an equally slippery and subversive figure. The doubling between these two characters reflects a deeper divide in the Zainichi Korean subject, who is always caught between Japan(ese) and Korea(n) and who does not fit easily into either category. In this sense, the real trickster in "The Trial of Pak Tal" is not Pak Tal; it is the Zainichi Korean narrator (or author) who straddles Japan(ese) and Korea(n) and thus has multiple identities and allegiances, much like a translator or a traitor, as in the Italian saying *"traduttore, traditore"* ("translator, traitor"). Indeed, in "The Trial of Pak Tal," the narrator/author (the line between the two is always unclear) ends up betraying the

12 Hirose, *Kimu Darusu to sono jidai*, 143–169. Also see: Hirose Yōichi, "Kimu Darusu 'Paku Tari no saiban,'" in *"Sengo bungaku" no genzaikei*, eds. Kōno Kensuke, Naitō Chizuko, and Narita Ryūichi (Tokyo: Heibonsha, 2020), 96–101. For more on *tenkō*, see: Yoshimoto Takaaki, "On Tenkō, or Ideological Conversion," trans. Hisaaki Wake, *Review of Japanese Culture and Society* 20 (December 2008): 99–119; and Yukiko Shigeto, "Tenkō and Writing: The Case of Nakano Shigeharu," *positions: asia critique* 22.2 (Spring 2014): 517–540.

THE TRIAL OF PAK TAL AND OTHER STORIES

readers at the end, refusing to tell us how Pak Tal's story ends and making us wait for his return.

"The Trial of Pak Tal" was a turning point for Kim's literature, in more ways than one. Not only did it represent a significant change in his literary style and his approach to Zainichi Korean identity, thereby anticipating later writers and activists who would try to envision a "third way" for Zainichi Koreans beyond the dichotomies of Japan/Korea or North Korea/South Korea, it also signaled a gradual shift in his work from the present to the past and from fiction to non-fiction.[13] In his later years, Kim stopped writing fiction and focused his efforts on researching ancient Korean culture in Japan, especially so-called "peninsular immigrants" (*kikajin*). He published the groundbreaking and long-running series *Nihon no naka no Chōsen bunka* (Korean culture in Japan) from 1970 to 1991.[14] While some might find fault

---

13 For more on the "third way," see: David Chapman, *Zainichi Korean Identity and Ethnicity* (London and New York: Routledge, 2008), especially Chapter 3. Also see: John Lie, Zainichi *(Koreans in Japan): Diasporic Nationalism and Postcolonial Identity* (Berkeley and Los Angeles: University of California Press, 2008).

14 Kimu Darusu, ed., *Nihon no naka no Chōsen bunka*, 12 vols. (Tokyo: Kōdansha, 1970–1991).

with Kim for turning away from contemporary political issues toward the distant past, his historical works should be seen extension of his fiction: both question what it means to be Korean in Japan, albeit in very different ways and very different periods. These continuities and discontinuities between the present and the past—or the blurred boundaries between fiction and non-fiction—are clearly visible in Kim's "Tsushima made," translated here as "All the Way to Tsushima," which was published in the April 1975 issue of the Japanese journal *Bungei* (Literary Arts). Based on two trips Kim made to the island of Tsushima in 1973 and 1974, this text incorporates many different voices, styles, and texts. Like Zainichi Koreans themselves, it defies categorization. Following Kim and his compatriots on their quest to see Korea from Tsushima, the narrative is a journey not only to the edge of Japan (or the edge of Korea, depending on one's perspective), but also to the heart of what it means to be Zainichi Korean. In this regard, it might be called a postcolonial rewriting of Matsuo Bashō's famous travelogue *Oku no hosomichi* (A narrow road to the far north) from 1702. The final scene, where Kim and his two friends climb to the top of Mt. Senbyōmaki and finally see their long-lost ethnic homeland, is one of the most moving and poignant in all of Kim's literature. On their way down from the summit, Kim wants to scream something out loud but does not know where or what to scream. His silent scream speaks volumes about the diasporic condition of being Zainichi Korean.

Kim died of liver failure on May 24, 1997, in a Tokyo hospital. He is buried in a cemetery at the foot of Mt. Fuji, forever in the shadow of Japan's most iconic mountain. Looking back on his long and illustrious career, three things stand out. First, Kim was an exceptionally talented and versatile writer. From the dense psychological descriptions in "Kindred Spirits" to the detailed historical references in "All the Way to Tsushima," the works in this collection reveal a writer who was not only a literary prodigy in Japanese—having picked up the language, quite literally, as a trash collector at a young age—but who also constantly questioned and expanded what it means to write in Japanese as a non-Japanese. In this regard, he was a forerunner of the genre now known as *Nihongo bungaku* (Japanese-language literature), represented by writers such as Levy Hideo, Tawada Yōko, and many others. Second, Kim depicted many different kinds of Zainichi Koreans and others in his work. The stories in this collection feature a wide range of memorable characters—both Japanese and Korean—from all walks of life and various political persuasions. Together, they represent a diverse cross-section of society, thus challenging the myth of Japan as monoethnic and the image of Zainichi Koreans as monolithic. Third, and perhaps most important, Kim tried to humanize Japanese-Korean relations.[15] While he never forgot the painful histories of colonialism, racism, and nationalism that have divided Japan and Korea or Japanese and Koreans, he used his sense of humor and his interest in human nature to highlight the human connections between them, emphasizing their shared humanity over their mutual hostility. In this way, he saw Japanese and Koreans as fundamentally kindred spirits. In addition to introducing Kim's work to a wider audience and raising awareness about Zainichi Korean issues in general, I hope that this translation also contributes to greater understanding and communication between Japan, North and South

---

15 Hirose Yōichi, "Kaisetsu: Ningen teki na Nitchō kankei no kōchiku ni jinryoku," in Kimu Darusu, *Kimu Darusu shōsetsu shū*, 297–313.

THE TRIAL OF PAK TAL AND OTHER STORIES

Korea, and the United States—or, as Pak Tal might say, "japanamerikorea."

Kindred Spirits

(*Takuju no kanpai*, 1948)

Well, he finally found me, An Tong-sun thought as he put the receiver down and stared off into space. He stretched out his hands on top of his desk and laced his fingers together, the same way he had when the air raids first began.

"*Kōyama.* Now that's a name you don't hear very often. Maybe he's secret police. He's not the guy who came here the other day, is he?" Sugai asked as he cleaned up his desk and got ready to go home. He was the branch editor who had answered the phone.

"No, that was Kōno."

"Hmm, they just keep coming one after another, don't they?"

As he said this, Sugai put down his thick glasses, pulled out his bento box from the desk drawer, and tucked it away in his bag. It may have been an offhand remark, but the normally prudent and fastidious Sugai sometimes made obnoxious comments like this, which were completely unbecoming of a newspaper reporter.

An Tong-sun, his hands still folded, could imagine the expression on Sugai's face without even looking at him: a sidelong smirk on his lips, his nose wrinkled in disgust. Unable to gauge whether that comment was an overt jab at himself for attracting the attention of the Military Police's Special Higher Police Section, or whether it was directed at the guys who kept coming "one after another," An Tong-sun remained silent. You could never really tell if Sugai was trying to be ironic or annoying.

"You don't mind if I leave, do you? This doesn't have to do with the paper or anything like that, does it?" Sugai asked as he re-tightened his gaiters and stood up with his bag under his arm.

"No, not at all. Please, go ahead. Also, just so you know, the call just now was from a Korean. Kōno said they got a new Korean recruit the other day, so he probably just wants to meet with me or something."

"Oh, I see. Maybe you're right."

Sugai looked a little surprised, but he brushed it off as

no big deal and headed out. In front of the door, though, he turned back for a moment, as if he wanted to get something off his chest before he left, and said, "Still, I'd rather you not meet with those kind of people at the office if at all possible. Not that I have anything against them or anything."

"No, neither do I . . . ."

It's not like I'm meeting with them because I want to, An Tong-sun wanted to add, but he stopped. After all, he was the one to blame for the whole thing, including what Sugai had just said to him.

Besides, he would have felt the same, whether the person was Korean or Japanese. If anything, the fact that it was a Korean only made that feeling more acute and oppressive for him. Nonetheless, he suddenly hated himself for saying, "Also, just so you know . . ." even though he had said it to smooth things over with Sugai, who did everything by the book.

Once Sugai had gone out the door and disappeared from view, An Tong-sun reflexively stood up and tried pacing around the room. But he soon gave up and went back to his original seat and sat down. *Well, he finally found me,* he thought again, more slowly this time.

"What an idiot. Calling me up at my office and telling me he's coming over. 'I'd like to come by in a little bit. Will you be there?' What kind of cop says that? If he wants to see me, he can come over to my house anytime he goddamn pleases. Be my guest, idiot," An Tong-sun muttered out loud. As he did so, he felt a heavy anger fill his chest.

Pressing his hands together more forcefully, he stared at the wooden wall in front of him, as if to quell his anger. On the other side of the wall was the office of the Fuel Control Joint Sales Association. A young war widow worked there by herself. She commuted from a town far down the coast and always wore baggy work pants with a matching jacket in a splashed pattern. She was a quiet woman, the kind who always seemed to be sitting still. Everyone called her "Ikeda-*san*." As An Tong-sun recalled this random woman, he spat out the word "goddamn dog" in Korean in a fairly loud voice.

"I haven't done anything wrong, and now this goddamn dog is on my tail. And an MP dog at that . . . ."

While he still had the chance, An Tong-sun wanted to say out loud the things that he surely would mumble to himself in his heart once that guy finally showed up to talk to him.

"You goddamn dog!"

However, he immediately burst out laughing by himself. Hearing his own laughter suddenly made him laugh again. The idea of wanting to say things out loud while he still had the chance was so immature, and yet the fact that he immediately acted on that impulse was also funny to him, in a childish sort of way. All the same, his laughter had a hollow ring to it.

An Tong-sun already knew about Kōyama even before hearing about him from Kōno. "Oh, really now?" he had said to Kōno, but he had already heard about Kōyama from Ebara at the fire station and from Rim Chae-geun in the neighboring town of U. Furthermore, by that time, word of Kōyama had already spread like wildfire among the Koreans living in this part of Y City.

About twenty days earlier, the coastal village had raised quite a ruckus because of him. It was after noon, but the air-raid warning had been lifted, so the local *ajumeoni* (Korean aunties) were out by the water pipe doing laundry and preparing dinner in case of another air-raid warning. Then, out of nowhere, he showed up in plain clothes. He just stood there watching the *ajumeoni* go about their business. One of the *ajumeoni* from Chŏlla-do, who went by the name Chŏllado-ne (*ne* meaning "from" in Korean), noticed him. Taking down the laundry rod to cover up her voice, she calmly said in Korean, "*Aigu*, I think that guy's a *gaenom* (goddamn dog). Bun-ne, you better hurry and go clean up after those conscripts who've been drinkin'. And then go tell Grandpa or Grandma Sŭng-ik."

"Yeah, she's right. He sure is."

The other *ajumeoni* gathered together to block his line of sight and nudged Bun-ne. Playing it cool, Auntie Bun-ne left her laundry where it was and tried to slip away and go back inside. But he kept standing right behind her, according to the *ajumeoni*.

Auntie Bun-ne was so flustered that she forgot where she was going and just stood there facing forward, her body beginning to tremble. Chŏllado-ne, who first spotted the "*gaenom*," turned pale and dropped the laundry rod.

"Come on, *ajumeoni*, let's take a little walk," he said, pronouncing the Korean word *ajumeoni* very clearly and in the standard dialect of Keijō (Seoul) no less.

That's all it took. The village quickly erupted into the usual uproar that befell it every so often. At times like this, the villagers would grovel to the authorities on the one hand by brandishing the only weapon they had—the act of apology—while on the other hand cursing them to no end and calling them all kinds of names in Korean, which the police didn't understand. This time, however, even though their opponent was alone, he knew Korean, so that wouldn't work. Instead, all they could do was stand there slack-jawed in amazement. When Grandpa Sŭng-ik, who got the nickname "Tin Can" from his caustic big mouth, came running over and blurted out one of those insults, he was yelled at in Korean—a curt "What'd you call me?"—leaving him wide-eyed and speechless.

Kōyama lined up the Korean conscripts who'd been drinking illegal *t'akchu* at Bun-ne's house and gave them each a slap on the face.* In the end, he made two of the

---

* *T'akchu* (濁酒), also known as *doburoku* or *dakushu* in Japanese, is a kind of homebrewed rice wine. During and after World War II, especially during the early years of the Occupation period (1945–1952), many Zainichi Koreans and Japanese brewed and consumed this banned beverage, leading to increased police surveillance and prosecution of bootlegging and other illegal activities. In this regard, it is similar

Kindred Spirits

conscripts drag out the jugs of *t'akchu* from Bun-ne's house and Grandpa Sǔng-ik's house. Afterward, he made Grandpa and Grandma Sǔng-ik and the widow Auntie Bun-ne kneel on the ground before taking them to task, forcing them to apologize in front of the huge crowd by saying "I will never make it again" a hundred times each like a chorus. Despite Grandpa and Grandma Sǔng-ik's pleas, he ordered the two conscripts to dump a total of two-and-a-half tubs of *t'akchu* into the ocean. Even while being subjected to this kind of abuse, none of them were brave enough to ask the guy who he was or where he came from, so after it was all over, they had a child follow him home and found out that he went into the Military Police headquarters, after giving a quick salute at the gate.

That night, about an hour later, An Tong-sun heard the whole story multiple times from various people. As usual, the most dramatic of all was Kunimoto Mitsuhide, also known as Ri Sam-su, the flag-bearer for the local branch of the Civil Defense Corps in the lower landfill village. He rushed over to break the big news in his Civil Defense Corps uniform, which he was so proud of because he'd

---

to *kasutori* (homebrewed *shōchū*), which was also criminalized and stigmatized after World War II. [Translator]

THE TRIAL OF PAK TAL AND OTHER STORIES

recently been promoted to two stars, thus exempting him from the draft.

"But even a Japanese person who's been to Korea would know that much Korean. Plus, there are tons of Japanese people with Korean-looking faces," An Tong-sun said.

This time, Sam-su and everyone else were more concerned about the fact that the MP knew Korean and seemed to be Korean than that he'd busted them for bootlegging, scolded them, and thrown their jugs into the ocean. The upper coastal village and the lower landfill village—this is what people habitually called them, even though they were both basically slums built on reclaimed land by the coast, with An Tong-sun's house located halfway between them—had been subjected to random blanket searches by Military Police officers on a few occasions, completely upending the lives of the residents. The MPs had confiscated jugs and other equipment for preparing *t'akchu* as accessories and had dragged some people out and handed them over to the police, slapping them with fines from the tax office or the courthouse and even sending some of them to prison in the end—despite An Tong-sun's efforts to intercede on their behalf—but they'd never done anything this severe before.

"No, no, really, I'm telling you the truth. Okay, sure, maybe the only Korean words out of the guy's mouth were 'ajumeoni' and 'What'd you call me?' But Grandpa Sŭng-ik, you see, wanted to test him, so when he said, 'I will never make it again,' for about the seventieth time out of a hundred, he tried saying the rest in Korean. Apparently, the guy just listened without saying a word," Sam-su said, sticking by his theory that Kōyama was Korean.

An Tong-sun burst out laughing at the part where Grandpa Sŭng-ik was left speechless after accidentally bad-mouthing the guy and then getting yelled at in Korean, and he laughed out loud again at the part where Grandpa Sŭng-ik tried to test the guy even while being chewed out, but actually he was deeply troubled by the possibility that the guy might be Korean. If that were true, then the guy probably wasn't there to crack down on things like bootlegging, which fell under the jurisdiction of the civilian police.

"Hmm, if that's the case, then . . ." An Tong-sun said, turning away.

"That's what I'm telling you—we're screwed. If that guy

really is Korean, then we won't be able to survive. He'll probably go around trying to sniff out every little thing that we're doing. Those goddamn dogs are all the same, but the Korean ones piss me off even more. Now we've got two damn dogs on our tails, if you count that bastard Maruyama who calls himself secretary or whatever of the Harmonization Society even though he's a fuckin' cop. What's worse, this guy's an honest-to-goodness MP, which is much scarier than the police. By the way, I meant to ask you this earlier, but are Koreans even allowed to become MPs?"

"Yeah, I was wondering the same thing myself, but, you know, the House of Peers or whatever it's called just passed a bunch of special measures or something as part of some welfare improvement program or whatever they call it. I don't know much about it, but maybe they made a special exception or something and changed the law. But they've had Korean MPs in Korea for a while now, so maybe they've had them here, too."

"I dunno what's so special about it, but it ain't gonna help us out one little bit. Who the hell would want special permission just to become a goddamn dog?"

"You should stop brewing so much illegal *t'akchu*.

Then maybe you wouldn't be so bitter," An Tong-sun laughed, amused by Ri Sam-su's growing agitation, which seemed out of character for a Civil Defense Corps branch flag-bearer.

"I'm not kidding. If they take away our *t'akchu*, that's it. There's no way we can survive. You of all people should know that. It's just like you said at the tax office last time, when you used all those smooth words of yours. The only reason why we Koreans are so good at digging those air-raid shelters and all the other jobs the Japanese aren't strong enough to do is because of chili peppers, garlic, and *t'akchu*. Plus, people say shit like 'We're at war' and 'We're doing it for the nation,' but it ain't our war and it ain't our nation. You're gonna get mad at me for saying this, but our neighborhood association is pretty much done digging all the underground tunnels, so recently I've been thinking I might try my hand at making candy or something."

"Come on, now, that's no way for a two-star Civil Defense Corps branch flag-bearer to talk!"

"Cut it out, I'm not kidding. I have two words for you: the draft. How would you like it if I was dragged off to the South Pacific and blown to bits? By the way, that reminds me—you probably know this already, but the number of Korean conscripts from the countryside has really shot up recently. These guys get dragged all the way over here to Japan, but when they try a cup of our *t'akchu*, they can't get enough of the stuff. The other day, these two guys who came to Grandpa Sŭng-ik's place just sat there staring at their drinks, without even drinking them, and whimpering like little babies. Now I don't miss a single thing about Korea, but these guys couldn't stop blabbering about how much they miss their homeland. Idiots. If they miss Korea so much, why were they dumb enough to get drafted in the first place? They could've just run away somewhere or done something to get out of it. Anyway, Grandpa Sŭng-ik—that old loudmouth everyone calls 'Tin Can'—suddenly shut up and got to thinking. After all, he came to Japan, too, with a bunch of his fellow countrymen. Then he announced that he was gonna give all 'fellow Korean' draftees regular cups of *t'akchu*—in other words, the same amount you and I drink—for half off, which ended up getting him into a huge fight with his old lady . . . ."

As usual, Sam-su began to prattle on, his voice full of bluster. Normally, An Tong-sun enjoyed Sam-su's gift of gab, sometimes even egging him on, but now he listened to him out of one ear, his mind increasingly preoccupied with an acute thought.

An Tong-sun knew about the draftees. There was a particularly high number of them here in Y City because of its status as a special military city. Although he had no way of knowing their exact number, since so many of them had been mobilized almost overnight due to the construction of military facilities in and around the city, they probably numbered in the thousands. Dressed in shabby khaki-colored tops and bottoms, they stood out like a sore thumb on the city streets, which were now largely empty of men. He had also heard about their ties to Grandpa Sŭng-ik. Even without a lecture from Sam-su about the necessity and significance of *t'akchu*, An Tong-sun knew all too well—as a Korean himself—how hard it was for them to give up that taste of home in this foreign land, where they shared a fateful, delicate bond. If Kōyama really was a Korean "dog," and if he decided to use his Korean eyes to search out and expose the underlying resourcefulness of these Koreans, who were just trying to make a living after many years of being unable to hold steady jobs under a relentless wartime economy—not only by bootlegging *t'akchu* but also by using their dubious wits to cobble together the scraps that fell to the bottom of that same economy—then there was absolutely no way they could survive, as Sam-su had said. Out of impatience with an endless war that had become a losing battle as the days wore on, the lives of these Koreans absolutely deserved to be exposed. The more they deserved to be exposed, however, the more An Tong-sun wanted to cover them up and protect them out of a strange urge that arose within him. That urge did not simply come from his own intentions or from the instincts of someone set adrift in a foreign land. It was a parasitic group mentality. By waging an unending war of its own making, Japan was forced to live with this group of parasites that clung to its side like mites it could never pluck off. For these "parasites," the act of clinging was itself a form of fighting.

But now their very existence was threatened by the appearance of that guy. They weren't the only ones threatened, though. This was also a pressing issue for An Tong-sun himself, who was directly involved. After all, it takes a Korean to know a Korean—and to find one!

It was probably around the beginning of the Pacific

War, An Tong-sun recalled—around the time he got a
job with a local newspaper in this city—that he began
to sense those cold, dark looks from the secret police.
Those looks gradually got stronger as the war progressed.
First, his friend from school and his older brother were
arrested. Then Kim Chin-chu, who raised pigs deep in
the hills behind the city, was arrested, as well as another
older friend. An Tong-sun himself had his bookshelves
ransacked by a secret police detective who demanded
to see his diary, which he'd already burned along with a
number of other things. He avoided visiting or writing
to his friends in Tokyo and Keijō (Seoul) without talking
about it with them beforehand. An Tong-sun tried to stay
in Y City as much as possible, but on those rare occasions
when he went to neighboring Tokyo for the day, the
secret police chief—whom he saw on a daily basis as a
reporter assigned to the police station—would ask him in
a roundabout way where he'd gone and what he'd been
doing there.

Living each day surrounded by such watchful eyes, An
Tong-sun sometimes nervously and other times almost
despairingly thought he might be arrested. Apart from
just one thing, however, there was hardly any reason

THE TRIAL OF PAK TAL AND OTHER STORIES

whatsoever for him to be arrested and shuffled around from one holding cell to another for months or years on end. Even when he imagined himself getting arrested and being left to rot in a cell, it didn't seem so painful compared to the slow suffocation of being surrounded by those cold eyes all the time. Still, when he thought about it like that, he was tormented by how easily he could be arrested, and by how little justification there would be for doing so.

True, when Kim Chin-chu was released on parole two years ago and had to get permission from the police to go just about anywhere, An Tong-sun was the one who had made Kim a fake employee ID card from the newspaper and had helped Kim escape by pulling some strings with the station master to procure a ticket for Kim to cross the Genkai Sea to Korea. For An Tong-sun, that alone didn't warrant an arrest. For those guys in the secret police, though, that was all the reason they needed. To begin with, they had no compelling reason to arrest his older brother, his older friend, or even Kim Chin-chu. They were the ones who decided who got arrested and why, not the other way around. An Tong-sun knew that everything depended upon their utterly self-centered intentions, which included their calculations, their sentimental favoritism, their flawed judgment, their petty reasons, and their overall personal situations—all of which could never be criticized. The only thing they cared about was scoring points or achievements for someone higher up the ladder. That was their system. And this warped system was highly developed. Still, though, the people in that system had to be human beings.

An Tong-sun discovered this through his own work in no time. Thus, his job as a newspaper reporter quickly came to acquire a kind of secret "self-awareness." In his scoops on the police, he learned to slip in the names of the relevant assistant police inspectors and detectives as much as possible. His regular fellow Koreans needed to know who the secret police were, of course, but also who the detectives from the Economic Security Section were. They also needed to know the public prosecutor and the judge from the local courthouse, to say nothing of the police chief. And it was absolutely necessary to know about the Labor Mobilization Office in case any of his fellow countrymen got drafted.

When the newly appointed secret police chief bragged about not bringing a bento box to work because he only ate two meals a day, An Tong-sun wrote this up in an article next to a photograph of the fat man. Of course, this was a bald-faced lie. When lunchtime rolled around, the chief went out every day with the other police chief to an off-limits restaurant in the neighborhood, where they ate much more than just a homemade bento box. To be polite, though, he wrote that the reason the chief went out to lunch was to leave his seat out of respect for his subordinates who used their own bento boxes. When there was an air raid, although it was immediately obvious that the target was military facilities for small carrier-based aircraft, he wrote at great length about how the police chief had "remained calm and self-possessed" while, in fact, the man remained glued to his seat, the color gradually draining from his face. Destined to a life of lowly jobs in the provinces until they died, and only concerned about doing their jobs faithfully and getting more and more brownie points, they had a desire for fame that was twice as strong as most people. Whether or not it would make them famous he didn't know, but they willingly provided him with articles in which they wanted their names and photographs to appear, sometimes secretly demanding that he print them. As he wrote these articles, An Tong-sun sometimes felt an impulsive desire to throw his pencil across the room or a nauseating kind of self-hatred, but other times he approached them as a form of "creative writing." His newspaper was a local paper under the so-called "one prefecture, one paper" model, where one edition served the entire prefecture. But because most of the reporters had been dragged off to the front, they were always short of articles, so these daily updates of his were almost never rejected. It must have been an odd sight indeed to see the pages filled day after day with so many of these articles about Y City, where An Tong-sun lived, even though there were plenty of other police stations, courthouses, and labor mobilization offices throughout the prefecture. He also made a concerted effort to get to know them better by playing along with their typically vulgar banter and never forgetting to laugh out loud with them at their jokes, even though he felt a part of himself dying inside.

Thus, by grasping the human rawness they revealed to him, along with their weak points, An Tong-sun softened their slightly cold gazes toward him. Still, in his heart, he felt as if he were walking a tightrope every day. The war was clearly nearing its end. Half of Tokyo was already in ashes. For the time being, his only wish was to survive until the end of the war—to make it safely to the end of this endless war by any means necessary.

Shortly thereafter, while he was busy dealing with the civilian secret police, the Military Police showed up out of nowhere. He had forgotten about them. One day, Kōno came by his house, handing him a name card with the title "Army Military Police Sergeant, Special Higher Police Section, Y Military Police Headquarters" on it. An Tongsun completely lost his composure. Come to think of it, he'd never given a second thought to the Military Police. Whenever he passed MPs on the street or rode the bus by their headquarters, which had a bus stop out front, he saw them wearing their white armbands dyed red with the big characters for "MP." They usually wore red leather boots with a long Japanese sword hanging pretentiously by their side. Every time he saw them, he felt an instinctive kind of fear—which came from being an oppressed minority— that naturally made him get out of the way, but he never dreamed he would become directly involved with them. Moreover, he'd heard that reporters used to visit this Military Police headquarters and conduct interviews there, but apparently reporters weren't allowed in anymore due to the new commander, who had taken over when the unit was raised to the status of a headquarters after the start of the Pacific War. Even if visits were permitted again, An Tong-sun couldn't imagine being able to go in and out as he pleased, no matter who he was. Now, he had no choice but to leave everything up to the intentions of his new opponent. Furthermore, when Kōno came a second time, he mentioned Kim Chin-chu's name and grinned, never taking those cold eyes off of him.

Then the other guy suddenly showed up. There was no doubt he was Korean. That was obvious just from his unusual Japanese name: Kōyama Ungi (黃山運基). From that point on, he came to occupy An Tong-sun's every waking thought. *He will definitely come*, he thought. He wondered how much Kōyama would scope them out with his "Korean vision." Or maybe he was scoping them out already. At any rate, he would come. The more he waited for him, however, the more he didn't show up. Kōyama visited Ebara at the fire station twice and Rim Chae-geun in U Town once. To make matters worse, he'd mentioned An Tong-sun's name to them, asking them point blank if they knew him. And yet Kōyama still hadn't come to see him directly. An Tong-sun pictured him in his mind almost every day, imagining all kinds of worst-case scenarios, eventually becoming more and more anxious. Come to think of it, he hadn't seen Kōno, either, since that last time.

It occurred to An Tong-sun that the military secret police might have made some kind of mistake in identifying him as a person requiring observation, so they were no longer interested in him. That thought alone filled him with a sense of relief. But it was only a temporary peace of mind. When he realized that, an even heavier anxiety came to weigh upon his shoulders. That's when Kōyama called and finally came over.

The long siren of an alert warning went off. When it ended, it quickly switched to the intermittent sound of an air-raid warning. The radio loudspeaker on the Waterworks Bureau across the street buzzed to life, announcing two or three P-51 Mustangs inbound from Iwo Jima. An Tong-sun stood up and went over to the door, pulling the black curtain two-thirds shut. The radio said the bombers were headed toward Y. After making sure he couldn't be seen from the outside, An Tong-sun went back to his original seat and sat down. Small aircraft might come close, but they were targeting naval facilities, so as long as you could avoid the shrapnel from the anti-aircraft guns firing randomly from the ground, there was no need to make a mad dash for the air-raid shelters. After so many air raids, An Tong-sun had developed nerves of steel. Even so, that didn't mean he was free to lounge around indoors, where people could see him from the outside. If he did that, the Civil Defense Corps would go crazy because they were afraid of him most of all. In particular, if a prejudiced person knew he was Korean and saw him doing that, they might suspect he was somehow communicating with the enemy aircraft. He couldn't let himself become too paranoid, but if he acted too calm at times like this, even Sugai would give him a look that seemed to say, "I guess those planes aren't necessarily bad news for you," and quietly sneak off to the air-raid shelter by himself.

By the whine that could be heard overhead, the planes had arrived. The anti-aircraft guns went off, exploding right above his head.

"Yikes, that was a close one," a man said, jumping in front of the door. As he looked up at the sky, he opened the door behind him and came in.

"Well, hello. If one of those bombs had fallen here and anything had happened to you, I guess it would be my fault, huh? I'm very sorry to have kept you waiting at the end of the day like this."

It was Kōyama.

An Tong-sun stood up from his chair and looked at him. He was a thin man of medium height. Ebara and Rim Chae-geun had said he was twenty-three or twenty-four, but he looked older than that. To An Tong-sun, he looked about thirty, only five or six years older than himself. He had a chiseled jawline. And the first words out of his mouth were pleasant enough. He came in with a cheerful attitude, using the air raid as an excuse to break the ice, but that wasn't such a bad way to begin, An Tong-sun thought.

"I see everyone has already left. Allow me to introduce myself . . . ." Kōyama said, pulling out a name card from the inner pocket of his black suit jacket.

As he always did when meeting another Korean for the first time, An Tong-sun felt an initial repulsion to Kōyama's use of Japanese and thought about replying in Korean, but he quickly scrapped that idea and replied in Japanese.

"Nice to meet you."

"I'm Kōyama."

An Tong-sun then introduced himself, offering his name card in return.

Sure enough, Kōyama worked for the Special Higher Police Section. His title didn't have a rank like "Sergeant," as Kōno's had.

An Tong-sun sat down and offered him a chair. Kōyama pulled it up and sat down right across from him.

"Looks like they're gone," Kōyama said.

"What? Oh, you're right."

Quickly realizing that Kōyama was referring to the enemy aircraft, An Tong-sun leaned forward and looked toward the window, pretending to look up at the sky, which he had no way of seeing from his position. Come to think of it, the crackle of the anti-aircraft gunfire had stopped. He'd completely forgotten about them since Kōyama came in. Or maybe they'd stopped the moment he came in.

Get a hold of yourself, An Tong-sun thought.

"So how many people work in this branch? It is a branch, right? Where's the main office? Is it that one over in Y, where the prefectural office is?"

Indeed, he seemed generally interested in the newspaper business, asking all sorts of questions as he looked around the room. There were only about five desks and five or six chairs scattered around the room and not much else except the usual things you would expect to find in a newspaper office. He was asking questions to make small talk. The all-clear siren sounded.

"That's right," An Tong-sun replied, as if to say, "I'd be happy to provide you with the correct information about anything of that nature."

"Before we merged with the prefectural paper," he continued, "our local paper, based out of this office, was more influential and had a higher circulation. For that reason, even as a branch office we had five or six people on staff at the beginning, but they gradually left—to cover the war and whatnot—so now it's just me and one other person, the branch editor."

"I see," Kōyama said and crossed his legs, showing off his red pigskin boots. As he looked around the room, he smoked a cigarette.

An Tong-sun also lit a cigarette, his last one. He had nothing in particular to talk about. An uncomfortable silence fell between them.

However, Kōyama was the one who had called and asked to come over. He was here because he had something to talk about or some other business to discuss. Awkward as he might feel, there was no need for An Tong-sun to worry about finding something to talk about. All he had to do was think about something else in the meantime. But An Tong-sun couldn't get his mind off of Kōyama. When Kōyama first came in, he was chatty and easygoing, but at base he seemed to be a man of few words. Besides, although he was the one who had called and come over, there was probably no need to think about him so antagonistically. There was no way to know what he might say next. In that respect, he was the main character now. He held the key to the story.

Had he said something like "I'd like you to come with me to headquarters for a little chat," then it was all over. They probably had plenty of reasons to arrest him, and not just for Kim Chin-chu's escape. After all, they were the ones who came up with the reasons. They could do whatever they wanted. As these thoughts crossed his mind, An Tong-sun felt like he couldn't take it anymore, so he broke the silence.

"So, shall I call you Kōyama-*san* or Hwang-*san*? I

heard that Ebara down at the fire station is actually named Ch'oe, but he chose the name Ebara because the two characters are the same ones in Kangwŏn-do, where he's from in Korea."

He regretted that the moment he said it. He was the only one who knew that Kōyama was Korean; Kōyama hadn't said anything to him yet about being Korean. *If I brought it up*, he realized, *that means I knew about it beforehand and was noticing it! To make matters worse, bringing up that extra stuff about Ebara was basically admitting that I knew about their meeting. And that's not all. If he asked me what my real name was, would I be able to explain my own secret to him?*

An Tong-sun's real name and his so-called "Japanese" name, which was basically a new surname and a different given name, were written with the same three characters: 安東淳. Except for a small group of his Korean friends, however, most people called him by his Japanese name "Andō" (安東), including at the office. His name cards were printed with a slight space between the first two characters and the last character so people would read his name as Andō Jun, in Japanese style. When writing or printing three-character Korean names, it was actually common practice to put an equal amount of space between the three characters. He'd learned this bit of wisdom from a certain Korean writer he'd gotten to know a few years earlier, when the writer was still living in Japan. When he first joined the newspaper, the managing editor looked at his resume and asked, as if it were the most important question in the interview, "Haven't you changed your family name yet? Don't you know that people from Korea are supposed to take Japanese names like ours?" So, he immediately gave the same reply that his writer friend had given.

The writer was named Kim Sa-ryang (金士亮).*
Once, when he was on a ferry on his way home to Korea, a detective asked him for his name card. When he presented his card, with the characters for his name printed the same distance apart, the detective gave him the third degree. "Why haven't you changed your family

---

* This is a thinly veiled reference to the real-life writer Kim Sa-ryang (金史良, 1914–1950), one of the first Koreans to write literature in Japanese. His debut work "Hikari no naka ni" (Into the light, 1939) was nominated for the prestigious Akutagawa Prize and inspired Kim Tal-su's own debut work "Ichi" (One's place, 1940), which is translated in this volume. Kim Tal-su was friends with Kim Sa-ryang and later helped edit Kim Sa-ryang's collected works in Japanese. [Translator]

THE TRIAL OF PAK TAL AND OTHER STORIES

name?" the detective asked. This happened during the implementation of the so-called Name Change Ordinance under Governor-General Minami, when it was starting to be enforced more widely. At that point, Kim feigned innocence and replied, "Why, my name is Kaneshi Ryō," pronouncing his name in Japanese style. When he told that story to An Tong-sun, they both cracked up.

Ever since then, An Tong-sun himself had gotten into the habit of going by his Japanese name, putting a little space between the first two characters and the last one. Apart from those times when something happened that made him think, "Hey, I'm not Andō Jun, I'm An Tong-sun," he often forgot about his own name. It could be read both ways, which was convenient. There was no real need to keep it a secret or anything, but he kept it that way, at least when it came to the Military Police and the civilian secret police. In his carelessness, he got nervous inside and felt as if he were about to lose his cool. At this rate, if Kōyama asked him about Kim Chin-chu, he thought he might completely panic and end up blushing or sweating, which had never happened with other Japanese police officers until that point. But Kōyama just sat there, smoking his cigarette.

Kindred Spirits

After glancing at An Tong-sun's face, he said, "Yes, my name is Hwang," pronouncing only his surname in Korean as "Hangu."

Then he asked, "May I borrow this for a moment?"

He picked up the telephone receiver on the table and asked the operator to put him through to the fire station. Apparently, the mention of Ebara's name had reminded him of some unfinished business he had at the fire station. An Tong-sun breathed a sigh of relief, happy to be off the hook, at least for now. Kōyama asked for Ebara.

"Ahh, Ebara-*san*, nice to see you the other day. Yeah, well actually . . ."

His Japanese was a little stilted. To An Tong-sun's ears, his pronunciation was not quite correct, and he still had a trace of a Korean accent.

"No, it's nothing in particular, I'm just over here at the newspaper office visiting Andō-*san*. Yes, yes, that's right. Are you on duty tonight? Eh? You're not—leaving—ah, you're about to leave? Oh really? Eh? You're coming over here? Oh really? Yes, he's here. Here you go."

Kōyama said the last bit to An Tong-sun and handed him the receiver. Putting it against his ear, he heard Ebara's usual chipper voice on the other end.

"Ah, *moshi moshi*. Hahaha, how's it goin'? Listen, don't go anywhere, I'll be getting off the boat soon, if you know what I mean. Let's go have a drink tonight, okay? Whaddya say?"

An Tong-sun was silent.

"Hahaha, come on, man. Look, I'll be there in a sec," he said and hung up.

"Well, hello there, my friends . . . ."

Ebara came over right away from the nearby fire station, wearing an assistant police inspector uniform with black gaiters and carrying a small canvas satchel. He was an assistant fire engineer, but his uniform was the same as that of an assistant police inspector, so his fellow Koreans jokingly called him "Mr. Inspector, Mr. Inspector."

"Kōyama-*san*, how about the three of us go out for a drink tonight to get to know each other better? Come on, it'll be fun. Shall we?"

Ebara stood at the entrance with a big grin on his face. When Ebara smiled, he looked as innocent as a child. He had an unusually carefree and sunny disposition for a Korean. It was also rare for a Korean to be a fire official. He'd been transferred to the fire station in Y City about seven or eight months ago, but he and An Tong-sun became fast friends through their respective jobs. One time, over New Year's, Ebara got drunk and piled An Tong-sun, Rim Chae-geun (who worked as a sign painter in town), and Ri Sam-su into his bright red fire engine, and they raced around town at breakneck speed. When he spotted some naval officers crossing the street, he deliberately turned the wheel toward them and screamed, "Watch where you're going, you idiots!" An Tong-sun was mortified, but it was a refreshing experience for him.

Kōyama just sat there with a faint smile on his lips.

"How 'bout it, An-*chan*, you're done for the day, right? Come on, let's go."

This time, Ebara called An Tong-sun by the nickname "*an-chan*" ("big bro"), which they used when they were drunk. An Tong-sun knew exactly what Ebara was referring to: their secret Korean brotherhood. It's why he'd used the phrase "getting off the boat" on the phone earlier.

"Sure," An Tong-sun said and prepared to get up. Kōyama promptly put away the box of cigarettes on the table and stood up. Then An Tong-sun stood up and followed him out.

Ebara waited by the door while An Tong-sun locked up. When he saw that Kōyama was out of earshot, he quickly said in Korean, "Let's take him down to the coastal village and give him a taste of our *t'akchu*."

The three of them boarded a bus and got off near the coastal village, one stop before the end. When the bus came to a stop, Ebara suddenly announced, "Come on, let's get off here." He stood up first and marched off the bus. An Tong-sun knew what was going on, so he quickly got off next, but Kōyama followed them off the bus somewhat reluctantly, not quite sure what he was getting himself into. They stood beside a narrow road running along the coast, on the edge of Y City's Korean enclave, more commonly known as the coastal village. When they began walking toward the village, the villagers quickly recognized them. An Tong-sun knew right away they were causing a commotion, from the way the people on the street darted back inside their homes. This became even more apparent the closer they got. The people who had run inside came out again to see what was going on, the *ajumeoni* disappeared down the alleyways between the buildings, and even the kids who had been playing on the street slowly clustered together, fixing their eyes on

65

them.

Over by the water pipe, where Kōyama had stood the other day, a group of *ajumeoni* was preparing dinner in silence, their faces downcast. One or two of them finally looked up and stared at Kōyama. The *ajumeoni* were huddled around the faucet, but there were some spaces between them, offering a few glimpses of cooking pots and jars used to pickle kimchi that had been left behind amidst the confusion.

Kōyama pretended not to notice and walked right past them, trying to look off into the distance. *I have to win this fight*, An Tong-sun thought. As he did so, he felt a power akin to courage well up inside him, but he pushed it back down, deep inside his heart. Suddenly, Ri Sam-su jumped out from a side alley right in front of them. He was wearing his usual Civil Defense Corps uniform, his face fire-engine red. Surprised to see them standing there right in front of him, he quickly pulled back. From the looks of it, he'd been drinking nearby.

"Hey, he-y," Ebara yelled, raising his hand to greet him, but Ri Sam-su ran back into the alley as fast as he could.

"Come on, let's go over here," Ebara said, suddenly marching off toward the village as they walked single file down the middle of the street. Now, even his voice was a little tense.

"Sure," An Tong-sun said a moment later.

Without even looking back at Kōyama, the two of them went straight into a house facing the street. It belonged to Chŏng "*Tangnagwi*," who always spoke in a hoarse voice, which he supposedly got from drinking a bowl of boiling hot tofu when he was young. *Tangnagwi* meant "donkey" in Korean. People with the surname Chŏng were nicknamed "donkey" because the left-hand side of the character for Chŏng (鄭) looks like a donkey's ears (奠).

They took off their shoes, stepped into the front room, and opened the window. Not surprisingly, Kōyama was standing in the middle of the street, lighting a cigarette.

"Hey, we're over here. Won't you come join us?" Ebara called out to Kōyama, leaning halfway out the window. Kōyama looked up at them with a sour face, but he walked toward them with an air of resignation.

When the three of them found a comfortable spot to sit in the room, the proprietor Chŏng quietly pushed open the wooden door to the kitchen in back and poked his head in, his jaw dropping in disbelief. He signaled to An

Tong-sun with his eyes. An Tong-sun stood up and went over to him.

"What the hell do you think you're doing?" "Donkey-Ears" Chŏng asked, lowering his hoarse voice in surprise. "Now, calm down, I take full responsibility for this. I'll pay you back later, but could you go over to Grandpa Sŭng-ik's and bring us a half-gallon of *t'akchu*?"

"Um, are all three of you drinking?"

"Of course."

"Donkey-Ears" Chŏng had seen a lot of things in his life. He immediately got the message and, with a knowing grin, ran out the door in a hurry.

When An Tong-sun came back, Ebara was smiling effusively, apparently chatting about something with Kōyama. The other man, however, was looking down with wrinkles at the corners of his eyes, trying to think of something as he exhaled smoke from his thick cigarette.

When An Tong-sun sat down, Kōyama turned to him and said, "I want to ask you two something. No, I want to ask you, Andō-*san*. What do you think about the way these people live?"

Kōyama stubbed out his half-smoked cigarette in the large bronze Korean ashtray.

An Tong-sun deliberately took his time before simply replying, "What do I think . . . ?"

"Come on, now, let's not argue. Why don't we save that for next time, shall we? Nobody lives like this because they want to. Anyway, save that for next time. You two just met each other today, right? There's no need to argue like that right off the bat. That's why I wanted to take you out for drinks today. We're all Koreans here. Let's just try to get along, okay?"

Ebara spoke quickly, waving both of his hands between them like a referee. "We're all Koreans here" was one of his favorite phrases.

"No, I wasn't trying to pick a fight with Andō-*san* or anything. I just wanted to ask your opinion, Andō-*san*."

Kōyama smiled begrudgingly. Smiling back, An Tong-sun suddenly thought, *I could knock him dead right here and now.*

"Oh good, the food's here," Ebara said, taking off his coat jacket and side sword and hanging them on the wall. Rolling up his shirt sleeves, he headed toward the kitchen door. The wooden door was quietly swinging open again, pushed by someone carrying a small table.

"Wow, this is amazing. Where did you find this? I

haven't had this in a long time. Hold on, just put it down there. Hey, An-*chan*, look, it's *ttongch'ang*!"

Ebara took hold of the small round table, which was halfway through the door, and placed it in the center of the room. On the table was a plate of *ttongch'ang* (giblets or, more commonly, guts) and a small charcoal brazier for grilling them. The coals were red-hot. Apparently, someone had just been grilling with it because the strong smell of grilled *ttongch'ang* rubbed with garlic and miso hit their noses. It was something that all Koreans loved, a smell that aroused a hunger deep in one's belly.

After Ebara put the small table down on the floor, he remained standing, encouraging the other two to come to the table. An Tong-sun knew what Ebara was up to, so he quickly sat down at the table. Trying not to look at the table, Kōyama pulled out another cigarette.

"Kōyama-*san*, won't you join us? Please, come over and have a seat."

Kōyama hesitated, so Ebara took the lead and sat down at the table. He put the mesh grill on top of the charcoal brazier and picked up some meat with his chopsticks, placing it on the grill. The *ttongch'ang* sizzled, suddenly filling the air with smoke and a pungent smell.

With his cigarette between his lips, Kōyama shifted his knees and slid over to the table. Ebara grabbed a piece of meat and popped it into his mouth.

"Ummm, that's so good. Hey, An-*chan*, grill some. Kōyama-*san*, please put some on the grill."

Kōyama picked up his chopsticks, peering at the meat. Just as they thought, he appeared to take a deep gulp.

"Wait a minute, we're missing the most important thing," Ebara said and stood up to go to the kitchen.

"Now we're talkin'! After all, you can't have *ttongch'ang* without this," he said to himself as he came back in with three bowls in one hand and a blue bottle of *t'akchu* in the other.

An Tong-sun pretended not to notice him. As he picked up some meat and ate it, he thought, *I could knock this guy dead right here and now.* Ebara gave them each a bowl and filled it to the brim with *t'akchu*, starting with Kōyama's. The man was chewing on some meat, also pretending not to notice. *Okay, I'll tell you what I think about the way these people live,* An Tong-sun thought. When Ebara finished pouring their three bowls, he picked up his and said in a slightly melancholy voice, "Let's drink, shall we?"

Kōyama, suddenly in good spirits, picked up his bowl at the same time as An Tong-sun. Then he stuck out his neck and took a sip. An Tong-sun drank all of his in one gulp. Ebara also emptied his bowl. Kōyama only drank a third of his.

The three of them looked at each other. Ebara burst out laughing.

"Hahahaha. Come on, let's be friends. We're all Koreans here, aren't we . . . ?"

"I guess this means Kim Chin-chu is gone for good, huh?" Kōyama muttered sullenly, taking a piece of meat and chewing on it as he washed it down with the *t'akchu* left in his bowl.

The Trial of Pak Tal

(Paku Tari no saiban, 1958)

The town of K in southern Korea is a pretty interesting place. Apparently, the capital of the governorate in Russia where that middling Collegiate Councilor Pavel Ivanovich Chichikov rode up out of nowhere on a barouche a hundred-some-odd years ago was also pretty interesting, but this town would give that one a run for its money any day.

Unfortunately, this town is not the capital of a governorate—or a province, in this case—but it is a respectable city of about 30,000 people. Not only does it have a local branch of the district court, but it also has a police station, of course, and a regional branch of the public prosecutor's office, as well as a prison. In this regard, it is exactly the same as the capital of that governorate Chichikov rode into all those years ago, but it differs from Russia in almost every other respect.

For one thing, this is present-day South Korea, the Republic of Korea, a far cry from the dark days of Russia before the emancipation of the serfs. Another difference is that the American military, the protector of the free world, has a base here. And besides, dear reader, I have no desire to introduce another man like the hero portrayed in *Dead Souls* by that Ukrainian writer Nikolai Vasilievich Gogol.

First of all, there cannot possibly be men walking around these days buying up dead serfs like Chichikov did. Plus, the hero of Gogol's story was a sixth-ranked member of the nobility, whereas the hero of our story is nothing more than a man who used to be a serf himself: a mere—and I do mean mere—farmhand named Pak Tal. Also, while that rascal Chichikov rode up out of nowhere on a barouche, our hapless hero is just about to be released from prison in K City.

In other words—and here, dear reader, is where our story really begins—he just got out. Our hero Pak Tal has just been thrown out from the back door of K Prison.

He stood there for a moment, looking around as though he'd forgotten something, and squinted his eyes, gazing down at the town quietly basking in the early summer sun.

Oddly enough, for someone who had just gotten out of prison, our hero wasn't very thin—which is not to say he was fat, either—but he was a pretty handsome guy, standing about six feet tall with a large build.

The rest of him, however, left something to be desired. The next moment, he stuck out his thumb and brought it to his face, blowing the snot out of one nostril with a trumpeting sound. Then he gave one more toot with the other nostril, using his middle finger this time.

He looked back at the black concrete walls of the prison he'd just left. "Eh-heh-heh," he almost chuckled in spite of himself, but then he wriggled his freshly cleared nostrils and snorted, "Hmph!" What did he mean by that? With just these few gestures, he left the prison on the hillside and headed into town with a surprisingly light gait for someone of his size. Without looking back, he marched straight down the main road into town.

Yes, that main road. This town known as K City is pretty interesting even in terms of its basic layout. That's not to say it's particularly unusual or anything, but the town is centered around a single main road that begins at

The Trial of Pak Tal

the front gate of the prison, which is the largest building in town.

The road is shaped like the character ㅏ, as in the element on the right side of the character for Pak (朴) or the *katakana* for *to* (ト). If you start with the prison here at the top, you draw a line straight down from the front gate and then flick your brush off to the side, as if to say, "To hell with the rest of it." Soon, you come to a place where the road splits like a hook toward the train station on the right. The area around this three-way junction is the government office district, where a bunch of buildings are clustered: the Local Branch of the District Court; the Public Prosecutor's Branch Office; the Police Station; the U.S. Military Headquarters, which also oversees the defense forces in this town; the Military Police; the Tax Office; the Labor Procurement Management Office; and the Municipal Office. This part of the road is also paved with asphalt, but only here.

Needless to say, this area is where the Japanese lived a long time ago, when they came here and brought the prison with them, so it was commonly called Japantown. Now, though, the area is home to a bunch of South Korean landowners and officials in charge of the government offices and then those guys—the Americans.

I must add a few more words of explanation regarding this road. When you leave the paved road—in other words, when you go past the middle of the character ㅏ—you enter a bumpy dirt road made of red clay that is unique to this region. The red clay has been trampled into a fine dust that often dances into the air. On either side of the road, appropriately enough, thatched-roof houses are packed tightly together, their low-hanging eaves brushing up against each other. Moreover, since this is a somewhat low-lying area, the round thatched-roof houses look just like clumps of mushrooms when viewed from the government office district on the right.

Needless to say, this is a small enclave of traditional houses within the town. Most have thatched roofs, but here and there you can see some with tin roofs and other kinds of roofs. In addition, this neighborhood also has things like loan associations, *kisaeng* (female entertainer) associations, and churches run by those Americans who do God's will by preaching that one must be patient in all things and that patience is a virtue. Basically, these places called churches are . . . no, let's get back to the main story.

Beyond this bumpy dirt road—in other words, when

you leave the city limits—you reach the outskirts of the town. Oddly enough, though, after the houses start to thin out, the road is paved in stately asphalt again for some reason. Farmers walk barefoot along it with their cows, watching out for the military trucks and jeeps that speed by. As you may have guessed by now, this road leads out to an airbase, which can't be seen because it's hidden behind a hill. The airbase belongs to the American military, which is in charge of guarding the country.

Well, that concludes our overview of the town, but let's see what our hero Pak Tal is up to. He has just passed through the paved section of the government office district and has reached the ト-shaped three-way junction that I mentioned earlier. By the way, the townspeople have a really good nickname for this part of town, but it doesn't quite translate into Japanese. If I had to translate it, though, it might be something like "Kowtown" (because of all the bigwigs there).

When Pak Tal came to the end of the paved road, he suddenly stopped again. What could he be thinking? He looked back at the government office district he'd just passed through. This time, he didn't blow his nose with his fingers, but he snorted again with a loud "Hmph!" He often had a strange way of laughing, but this time it felt a little more mischievous.

At that point, he finally set foot on the bumpy dirt road. Jeeps and other vehicles carrying American soldiers raced by constantly, stirring up dust in their wake. From out of those clouds of dust emerged an oxcart laden with night-soil buckets, lumbering toward him. And then a housewife, balancing a package from the grocery store on her head while repeatedly hitching up the child strapped to her back . . . .

Not a moment later, an old man with a long old-fashioned pipe in his mouth crossed the road. He was hunched over and clutching his pipe as if his life depended on it. Pak Tal nimbly weaved his way through these people as he strode down the street. Under his arm, he carried a small bundle wrapped in a dirty cloth. It was probably the coat or clothes he had been wearing when he was arrested by the police last winter.

All of a sudden, he slipped into a nearby alley and disappeared. Where in the world was he going? Here, we must wait a while for his return. After all, he walks frighteningly fast. It's hard to keep up with him. Besides, he's definitely going to show up in this town again.

Sure enough, when night rolled around, Pak Tal trundled up to a certain bar along the bumpy dirt road. Apparently, he hadn't gone home yet because he was still carrying the cloth bundle under his arm.

The bar was not the kind with a sign hanging out front. It was more like a local watering hole. From the fragrant smell that tickled his nose, he could tell they were cooking *gaejang* (dog soup) inside. As a member of modern, civilized society, I'm not very proud of the fact that the people here still eat dog in this day and age, but out of utmost consideration for the honor of my homeland, I must tell you the truth. Plus, *gaejang* was one of our hero Pak Tal's absolute favorite foods.

Pak Tal had already been treated to a hero's welcome of food and drink at each of the places he'd visited that day, but the smell of *gaejang* still made his nostrils twitch. He flung open the squeaky door, which often got stuck, practically knocking it down as he barged in.

From inside came a chorus of voices:

"Oh my gosh!"

"Well, if it isn't Pak Tal!"

"Hey, Pak Tal! You're still—wow, you made it out of

there alive."

The voices belonged to a group of guys whose faces were covered in grime—except their glimmering eyes—and whose heads were buried in bowls of *gaejang* that sat beside bottles of homebrewed *t'akchu*. They'd turned their heads around to look at Pak Tal standing in the doorway.

Pak Tal, though, just stood there for a while with a dumb grin on his face. It was unclear whether or not he'd heard them. One of the men offered him a seat, so he went over and sat down.

Still grinning, he turned to the guys on either side of him and looked at the bowls of *gaejang* on the wooden tray tables in front of them, as if to say, "How is it? Is it good? Man, that looks good."

The men were all laborers at the American military base. Crowding around Pak Tal, they kept gushing about how surprised they were to see him. A young woman swiftly ran out from the back, flashing a set of pearly white teeth. Apparently, she'd overheard them talking. When she spotted Pak Tal sitting there, she swiftly ran back into the kitchen. This was Tan-sŏn, who worked there as a cook and who (I guess you could say) was Pak Tal's wife.

Before long, she returned with a block of fresh tofu on a plate and plopped it down in front of Pak Tal. She stood there smiling, showing no particular expression on her face except for the gleam from her dark eyes and her pearly whites. When Pak Tal looked up from the plate of tofu and saw her, he only gave a little grin as well. Their looks suggested that they saw each other all the time, day in and day out. In fact, though, they hadn't seen each other for more than half a year.

"Wow, leave it to Tan-sŏn to remember the tofu. When you're done with that, try this next. It'll make you as good as new," said Old Man Cho Sŏk-u next to him. The old man pushed the bowl of *gaejang* he'd been about to eat in front of Pak Tal.

"Pak Tal, have this one, too."

From both sides, people pushed their bowls toward him. Some of the bowls were half finished.

"Hey, don't do that! Let's get him a new bowl. If we all chip in, it won't cost a thing," said the so-called intellectual Ri Chŏng-chu.

"Hold on, fellas. No matter how good it is, I can't eat this much *gaejang* all at once. Plus, it's not like I was hurting for food in there like you guys," Pak Tal said.

His voice, though, sounded cheerful, as if he were getting revved up.

"Well of course you weren't! Why would you have to worry about food when you're in the big house all the time? In that sense, you're the same as those old farts in the hospital."

Everyone burst out laughing. Even the people who'd finished eating and were about to leave decided to stay for a while once Pak Tal came in. Of course, there were some people who didn't know him, but they sat there watching him and thinking, *I don't know who this guy is, but he seems like quite a character.*

With a wide grin on his face, Pak Tal began with the fresh tofu that Tan-sŏn had brought out for him. The reason they served fresh tofu to people who'd just came back from police custody or prison was because of a long-standing belief that the tofu would keep them from being put behind bars again.

I don't know where this belief came from, but there must be tens or hundreds of thousands of people in this country who have eaten tofu for that reason. And now, our hero Pak Tal was doing the same thing. Even though its efficacy for him had long since been shown to be questionable at best, here he was eating it again.

"By the way, Pak Tal, what kind of people did you meet this time? And are you planning to cause another disturbance, like you did last time?" said Old Man Cho, who was sitting next to Pak Tal and watching him eat. His tone was quiet and serious, befitting his age.

"What kinda people, you ask? Why, all sorts of people. Nobody announces that they're planning to cause a disturbance, but am I not allowed to plan one?" Pak Tal replied nonchalantly while sipping on his peppery *gaejang*. He didn't appear particularly thin from his time in prison, but his pale face had quickly regained its vitality after being out of the sun for so long, and sweat dripped from his forehead.

"No, nobody's saying you're not allowed to. That's up to you," replied the so-called intellectual Ri Chŏng-chu from behind them. The reason he was called an intellectual by his friends—making him a "so-called intellectual"— was because he was the only one among them who had graduated from an agricultural college. He had also been arrested before for helping organize a labor union. He was the same age as Pak Tal, around thirty.

"What the old man's really asking is who those people

were, not what kind of people they were. You were in the slammer for quite a while this time, so I'm sure they taught you many things," Ri continued.

"I haven't . . . been to the real part of the prison yet," Pak Tal said as he finished off the last drops of soup in his bowl while everyone watched him. "Up till now—and this time, too—I was in a place called a detention center. Then I got a suspended sentence, whatever that means. So, in terms of school, I guess you could say I finally made it to about seventh grade."

"Sheesh! There you go again, mistaking prison for school. Man, you never change. Hahaha . . . ."

"But it is a school. Now, as it was in the past, the only decent people in this country are the ones in prison. Plus, the only school we can actually attend is . . ."

"Yeah, yeah, yeah, we've heard that story a thousand times before. Even so, you're one hell of a lucky guy, aren't you? This time, I thought for sure you'd be sent to prison for ten years or maybe something worse, but you managed to get out without even going to trial," Ri Chŏng-chu said with an exaggerated sigh.

However, he wasn't unhappy that Pak Tal was back. That was clear from the way he sighed.

"It's not a matter of luck," Pak Tal said offhandedly again.

"Ok, then what is it? Do you mean those guys gave you special treatment or something?"

"Are you kidding me? There's no such thing as special treatment in a place like prison. However, I can 'make' them do that. That's up to me. And those guys are no match for somebody like me."

"What's that supposed to mean?"

Ri Chŏng-chu leaned forward, aware that he was speaking with Pak Tal on behalf of everyone there. Pak Tal, though, kept speaking, without really turning around, as if he were talking to himself.

"Nothing, really. I've said this before, but to put it more simply, it just means you and I are different people. If anything, you're a big shot. That's why you'll never beat those guys no matter how hard you try. You take yourself too seriously. But I'm not like that. For somebody like me, as I get passed around from the police to the public prosecutor and then to the court, I always run up against a tough opponent at some point."

"You mean the whole conversion thing, where you get on your hands and knees and say, 'I'll never, ever do it again'?"

"Hmph! Of course. If I want them to kneel at my feet, then I'll kneel at theirs. And what's wrong with that? At least I still have my head, right . . . ? Anyway, forget about it. It's my problem, not yours. So, how's life on the outside been treatin' you guys? Are you havin' fun every day?"

For some reason, Pak Tal was suddenly seized with anger and looked around at the guys in the room. They looked back at him, rolling their eyes in the dim glow of the limited-electricity lights. No matter whose face you looked at, not a single one of them seemed able to say they were satisfied or having fun.

How could they? For "even if you worked your tongue off" for a month, as the saying went, they still couldn't afford to buy one *to*, or about thirty pounds, of white rice. They didn't feel like eating white rice to begin with (because they couldn't afford it anyway), so they didn't care how expensive it got. But assorted grains like millet and barley were getting more expensive as well, and there was nothing they could do about it.

The common folk of my beloved Korea tend to exaggerate, using adjectives in the style of Li Bai's famous expression "white hair 30,000 feet long" (*baifa sanqian zhang*). The phrase "you couldn't afford to buy one *to* of white rice 'even if you worked your tongue off'" has a similar feel to it. Actually, though, that was not the case. In fact, it was quite the opposite.

That is to say, one *to* of white rice now costs more than 4,000 *hwan* in Korea. By contrast, the monthly salary of a police officer, which is considered a good job for a respectable *nari* (gentleman) in this country, is approximately 3,000 *hwan*. Furthermore, the character *hwan*, which appeared on the paper bills, was unfamiliar to many people here in Korea. People said that during the recent currency reform, they mistook the character *hwan* (圜) for the character *won* (圓), the former currency, because they printed the bills in America. Whatever you did, you had to be careful not to get ripped off—that's what the people of this town firmly believed.

At any rate, one has to wonder: how did those gentlemanly police officers afford to eat on that kind of salary? Well, to use a word that's going around in this country right now, it's called *sabasaba* (dirty dealing). They were stuffing their stomachs by making dirty deals. So, for those laborers who had neither the power nor the connections to make dirty deals, no matter how much they "worked their tongues off," there really was no way they could afford to buy one *to* of white rice. These days, if a couple of people worked so hard that their tongues actually did fall off, it wouldn't even make it into the newspaper. I don't know when this happened, but when people first used the phrase "even if you worked your tongue off" a long time ago, it probably carried with it a touch of hyperbole—maybe not quite to the extent of "white hair 30,000 feet long," but at least as much as "white hair 10,000 or 20,000 feet long"—but now that sense of exaggeration has completely disappeared.

As proof of that, people don't use the expression much anymore. To be sure, there are still some people who say it simply out of habit, but they are few and far between. Well then, what expression do they use instead? They sigh "Ahhh . . ." They just cradle their empty stomachs and let out a long "Ahhh . . ." Now, even in conversation, people don't make pointless complaints like "even if you worked your tongue off." The minute you say "Ahhh . . ." the rest is understood. Let's suppose someone asks you, "How are you doing?" All you have to do is say "Ahhh . . ." and either look back at them with a feeble gaze or look up to the sky in desperation. Then the other person would reply with "Ahhh . . ." Earlier, I said something a bit biased regarding how these people like to eat dog. However, their main source of nutrition was the *gaejang* they were lucky enough to come across every ten days or so. But even this was a splurge.

Everything had become a complete mess, especially since the last war. The only things that went up were troops and taxes, not jobs or wages. Back in the day, this town used to have some industries like a small fertilizer factory and a spinning mill, but now they'd been converted into barracks for the defense forces. Other than entering these barracks and becoming a soldier, the only place where the people who poured in from the nearby farming villages every year could find work was on the American military base doing odd jobs referred to as "labor." However, these jobs paid practically nothing—even compared to Japan, from what I hear—so who knows how or where they came up with these wages. Inflation was rising so fast that there were times when it made no difference if you worked or not; no one could afford anything anyway.

"Hmph! How can we expect to have any fun around here? As you can see, we're just barely scrapin' by," one of the men exclaimed, mimicking Pak Tal's tone of voice. He was a young man of twenty-seven or twenty-eight, sitting diagonally across from Pak Tal.

"You got that right," said Old Man Cho, sitting next to Pak Tal. "Those of us here on the outside are only living like this 'cause we can't die. I'd wanna live in the 'big house' like you, too, Pak Tal, if it weren't for those little brats of mine who keep begging for food all the time."

At that point, after finally seeming to grasp the meaning of the question Pak Tal posed (since no one had even anticipated a question like that), they began a loud and lively debate throughout the room about whether or not they were "havin' fun every day."

"Loud and lively" was the right way to describe it: exclamations like "Oh, come on!" could be heard over deep sighs like the usual "Ahhh . . ." Then, just as it was ending, someone tried to wrap things up with a phrase that you'd never expect to hear in a debate, at least in theory: "What the hell are you talking about, you fucking idiot?" Before long, a single intelligible voice burst forth from the clamor.

"Ah, to hell with it! I wanna hit 'em with somethin' big this time. That would sure as hell knock 'em off their feet.

The Trial of Pak Tal

That's about the only thing I can think of that would give us any fun."

It was the young man who had pretended to talk like Pak Tal earlier. As he spoke, he gave a big, powerful stretch and stood up. As if on cue, everyone started rustling around, getting ready to go home.

"Hey, wait a sec," Pak Tal said and held the man back. "You just said you wanted to hit 'em with somethin' big this time. What did you mean by that?"

"A strike, a general strike!"

"Oh, have you ever organized a strike before? You don't look familiar to me. Where are you from?"

"Yeah, I have," he said, sitting back down. "Right after I got back from the recent war. I was a factory worker at a munitions plant in Pusan. Mind you, it was a factory run by the Americans. Anyway, to make a long story short, that's how I ended up here. I'm Ch'oe Tong-kil, by the way."

"Ch'oe Tong-kil, huh? In that case, maybe you should try hitting them with another strike here."

"Here? You gotta be kidding me. How could we pull off something like that with a bunch of wimps who are afraid of even forming a union?"

"You've greatly underestimated them. How do you know they're afraid? If you found out they weren't, then would you be able to do it . . . ?"

Pak Tal stared at Ch'oe Tong-kil with a meaningful look in his eyes. Suddenly, as they sat facing each other, a single chopstick flew in between them from somewhere across the room, clattering to the floor. They raised their faces and turned around.

About the same time, the normally squeaky door slid open without a sound about three-quarters of the way, and two plainclothes cops poked their heads in. Everyone fell silent, some looking toward the door, some looking away. Then all of a sudden, Pak Tal let out a strange laugh, "Eh-heh-heh," and stood up from his seat.

"Gentlemen, how are you this evening? Care for a bowl of *gaejang*?"

Still smiling, Pak Tal lifted up an empty bowl of *gaejang* nearby for them to see.

Hearing that, one of the plainclothes cops got upset and tried to storm in. When he spotted Pak Tal, though, he seemed a little surprised for some reason. More flustered than angry, the plainclothes cop snapped, "It's almost curfew. Stop dickin' around and get outta here!"

With that, he backed out of the door and left. The minute the cops were gone, the whole room erupted in laughter.

"Hahaha . . . that was a good one. Offering *gaejang* to those 'dogs'!"

The proprietress—perhaps having overhead their laughter, or perhaps having been informed by one of the staff that some plainclothes cops were snooping around—ran out from the back in a tizzy, clutching the hem of her *ch'ima* (Korean skirt).

"My word, what are you guys still doing here at this hour? And with just one bowl of *gaejang* . . . ? You mean you've been sittin' here this whole time with just one bowl of *gaejang* . . . ? What are you tryin' to do, run me out of business here? Mercy me, mercy me . . ."

The proprietress seemed to have many more gripes up her sleeves that she wanted to air, but when she spotted Pak Tal, she froze, as though she'd seen a ghost. She raised her finger and pointed at Pak Tal in disbelief. For a moment, she just moved her lips, not making a sound.

"It's been a while, Madame," Pak Tal said, slowly bowing his head toward her.

Outside, it was a moonlit night. It was nearly eleven
o'clock already, the nightly curfew, so there wasn't a single
person on the road. There wasn't a single dog either,
perhaps because they'd all been eaten.

Nothing moved except for the occasional military
truck or jeep that came roaring along the road, shadowed
in moonlight, sending up clouds of dust as they did
during the day. The only people you might run into were
police officers on their nightly rounds, but Pak Tal wasn't
afraid of them in the least.

Holding Tan-sŏn's hand, he waited for a truck to pass
them from behind. When the coast was clear, he marched
out to the middle of the road, forcing the oncoming jeeps
and other vehicles to swerve around them. It was a risky
move, almost like a stunt, but Tan-sŏn liked this side of
Pak Tal, too.

"What time . . . today . . . what time did you get out? If
I'd known, I would've gone to meet you . . . ."

Tan-sŏn clutched Pak Tal's hand and snuggled up
against him. They'd arranged to meet after Tan-sŏn got
off work, and now they were headed to the rented room
where she lived. The cloth bundle Pak Tal had been
carrying under his arm during the day was now in Tan-

sŏn's other hand.

"Huh? Hmm. They let me out a little after noon, but I went around to a few houses delivering some messages from the guys on the inside. I had to take care of that as soon as I got out or I might change my mind later on, you know. After all, the outside world is a pretty fickle place."

"I suppose you're right. That stuff is important. But still, you don't often change your mind."

"Yeah. Not like you women do."

There was a pause, and then Pak Tal jumped into the air with an exaggerated shout. "Owwwch!" Apparently, Tan-sŏn had pinched his rear end. Yep, they were quite the lovebirds.

An American jeep drove by and hurled some kind of lewd comment at them. Pak Tal must have thought they were insulting him for not getting out of the way because he immediately stopped and looked back toward the jeep.

"You idiots!" he screamed at the top of his lungs. Perhaps he was trying to hide his embarrassment.

"You fuckin' idiots! This is our road!" he screamed again.

His gruff voice, which could hardly be called melodious, echoed into the night sky and reverberated around them. The jeep was already long gone.

They held hands again and walked a little farther, at which point they turned into a side alley. They stopped beside the gate to a fairly large house. That's where they lived: in a room Tan-sŏn rented in a gated row house.

The room was a *changpanbang* (a room lined with oiled paper) about fifty square feet in size. When they went in, Tan-sŏn first took a wet rag and wiped down every inch of the *changpan* (oiled paper) floor. Then she got out a pillow for Pak Tal and let him rest on the floor while she went outside, where she borrowed a big pot from the back and started boiling some water.

Pal Tal stretched himself out on the floor and gazed up at the dark ceiling, which had no lights or anything else. Outside the sliding paper door, he could hear the crackling of the firewood that Tan-sŏn was burning. The light from the flames flickered against the paper screen from time to time, illuminating his face.

In the dim light, Pak Tal's eyes were faintly wet with tears. What on earth could he be thinking about? This was quite unusual for him—to have tears in his eyes, that is.

What had brought him to tears? Had he been moved

The Trial of Pak Tal

by Tan-sŏn's kindness toward him, after living like a stray dog until then? Or had he been thinking about his odd life up until that point?

Mind you, he'd only just turned thirty-one. The end of his lifetime, which is what the word "life" implies, still seemed far away, but a life is still a life, even a partial one. Maybe there were times when he unintentionally reflected on his life all of a sudden . . . .

Ah, yes, while Tan-sŏn is boiling water outside— although I still have no idea why she would be boiling water at this time of night—let me take this opportunity to tell you a little more about our hero Pak Tal's "life," such as it was.

These long, drawn-out stories about the protagonist's past, which amateurish writers often include in their novels, are generally a bore. At this point, dear readers, you might be thinking, *Ah, not one of those again.*

However, when it comes to our hero Pak Tal, he is cut from a different cloth than the protagonists of all those other novels. Indeed, this part of the story constitutes the "heart of the matter." Whether or not it's interesting is impossible for me to say, but it simply won't do to leave it out.

Even in this town, nobody knew where the heck this character Pak Tal had been born. They didn't even know which Pak clan he belonged to. (Clans are still a pretty big deal in this country because the storied Jeonju Yi clan referred to the current president and his blood relatives.) To begin with, his real name wasn't even Pak Tal; it was actually Pak Tal-sam.

In the process of repeatedly being called Pak Tal (including his family name), though, he himself soon became convinced that his full name was Pak Tal. But he wasn't the only one who believed that. Even the police officers and the public prosecutor who questioned him called him that, and they were supposed to be terribly fussy about things such as names. Their conversations went something like: "Not you again, Pak Tal . . ." and "Yessiree!"

No one knew where he'd been born, but when August 15, 1945, rolled around, he was twenty years old and a farmhand for the Yu family, who lived on the outskirts of K City and were the biggest landowners in all of southern Korea. He hadn't become a farmhand at that time; he'd already been working for the Yu family from the age of five. He was an indentured servant, as it were, but he'd probably been born to a far-off family of tenant farmers who offered him to the Yu family as a substitute for rent. Then his parents no doubt sold their house, wrapped up their affairs, and moved to Japan or somewhere.

Even someone as ignorant and uneducated as Pak Tal vaguely understood that the seemingly endless war was finally over and that Japan had lost in the end, meaning that Korea, which had been controlled by Japan, would now become independent at last. He'd also heard that all the Japanese officials were gone and that the town had formed a People's Committee in their place, mostly made up of people who'd been in the town prison until recently. He also heard a rumor that the land belonging to the big landowners would be divided up among tenant farmers and farmhands.

Pak Tal wondered how they could do something so stupid or, rather, something so wonderful. However, when he saw how panicked Master Yu was after years of getting along so well with the Japanese officials, it appeared to be more than just a baseless rumor. The master became kinder than normal, acting strangely chummy toward Pak Tal and speaking to him more politely.

Seeing these changes, Pak Tal began to think that

the People's Committee back in town might actually be telling the truth. At the same time, he started to feel a little sorry for the master, to the point where he thought about remaining on the property in his previous position, even if the master lost his land.

As it turned out, though, there was no need for either of them to be so concerned. One day, a rumor started going around that the American military had come to town. Pak Tal and the others had never seen an American before, but when the Americans rode up to the master's place on their jeeps, which looked like little toys, the master burst out laughing.

This time, Master Yu started currying favor with the Americans instead of the Japanese, and his attitude changed again almost overnight. In other words, he quickly went back to his same old self, screaming things like, "Tal-sameeee! You little son of a pig! Stop sittin' around on your ass all day and get to work! Hurry up and clean up those bales of rice husks! And when you're done with that . . ." Only the master called him by his correct given name, albeit in the diminutive form "Tal-sameeee."

In response, Pak Tal snorted "Hmph!" under his breath. He wasn't sneering at the master's angry voice, which was always dotted with exclamation points. Rather, he was laughing about what might be called his own twist of fate.

About three years had gone by when Pak Tal's lot in life took a surprising turn. Indeed, the liberation of Korea on August 15, 1945, signaled a change for him as well. A rumor began spreading that guerrilla fighters, who had been active across the mountains of southern Korea, had infiltrated the area where Pak Tal lived. Master Yu's family hastily moved to town, giving strict orders to Pak Tal and the other farmhands and maidservants to look after the place while they were away. Pak Tal wondered what all the fuss was about, but he did as he was told and kept an eye on the master's house and estate as he went about his daily chores.

One day, however, Pak Tal was suddenly taken into custody and brought to the police station in town. The previous day, the military and police substation in Pak Tal's village had been attacked by the guerrillas, and the police suspected that Pak Tal had conspired in the attack. As a matter of fact, the other farmhands had disappeared almost overnight after hearing of the attack, but no one had even bothered to tell Pak Tal why they were leaving.

Without so much as being questioned, Pak Tal was thrown into a cell at the police station and left there for days. You see, at that time in particular—and even now, to some extent—police stations were full of such political prisoners and thought criminals. The police just assumed all they had to do was arrest them and throw them in jail, which meant that the prisoners were pretty much left on their own. After all, the police and the public prosecutor's office had enough on their plates already.

After about two months, Pak Tal was finally dragged out for questioning. For some reason, though, he kept his mouth shut the entire time, refusing to say a word. By this time, a momentous change had already taken place within him.

The police officers in charge of interrogating Pak Tal were surprised by how he just glared at them in silence. "Maybe this guy's for real. Maybe he's one of the leaders," they thought. So, as usual, they began torturing him. Lo and behold, though, Pak Tal showed no signs of breaking. In fact, for him, it barely even hurt.

You might find this hard to believe, dear readers, but that is actually what happened, so you'll just have to take my word for it. When they inflicted too much physical pain, he did shed tears like an ox, as one might expect from a person with such a large build. However, that pain was nothing compared to the memory of the countless whippings he'd gotten from the master over the years since he was taken into the Yu family at the age of five, or the times he'd been tortured with fire and water by the Yu family's eldest son, who later died of a mental illness.

Clearly, a big change was occurring within Pak Tal. To begin with, he'd never seen anything like a guerrilla before, nor did he even know what one was. Maybe he should have just told them as much, but Pak Tal didn't want to be released from the police station jail quite yet. Why on earth not?

In that jail, you see, he came into contact with the concept of society for the first time in his life. Up until that point, his life had consisted of nothing more than carrying buckets of night soil on his back and cultivating the fields with cows, plows, and hoes as his sole companions. His only human interaction to speak of had been the dirty conversations he occasionally had with his fellow farmhands or the maidservants.

First of all, he'd never been afforded the time or the opportunity to meet other people. When he happened to get arrested by the police and got his first look at the inside of a jail cell, he was surprised to find it packed to the gills with the kind of people he'd never met before— or, rather, the kind of people he normally would never have dreamt of meeting. Moreover, apart from the thieves, most of the other inmates were the kind of people known as intellectuals, and they taught Pak Tal many things. At first, he was surprised to find so many smart people in a place like that, but all the things they taught him—the fact that the earth is round, for example—were the most precious things he'd ever heard.

This is probably what it means to experience an awakening. In Pak Tal's eyes, that jail seemed like a treasure house of knowledge about everything he'd been unable to learn in his life until that point. That was where he first learned why Korea was divided along the 38th parallel and what a guerrilla really was. He also learned what a landowner was. And it was from this time that he began "volunteering" to go to jail.

By the time he came home after being released from custody for his connection to the guerrillas (which was indeed the case), Pak Tal had of course been fired by the Yu family. Even if they hadn't fired him, he had no intention of going back to their house, so he came into town and became a jack-of-all-trades and a miscellaneous laborer.

Thus, he began a cycle of doing anything he could to get arrested and go back to jail. At the same time, as he did this over and over again, he became buddy-buddy with the police officers.

Getting arrested was easy. He could do that anytime he wanted. For instance, even when he was walking around town, if he suddenly felt like getting arrested, he could stop right there and try to deliver a little speech. That's all it took. It didn't even have to be a speech. All he had to do was shout one of those slogans he'd been taught in jail, like "Don't listen to what those tools say—they're puppets of America!"

If that didn't work, he would play his trump card and start talking about "socialism," another thing he'd learned about in jail. That always did the trick. The police would run right over, chase away the crowds, and do him the favor of arresting him. Sure, he got punched and kicked a little, but that sort of thing was no big deal for him anymore.

The same could be said for punishment and torture,

which he had plenty of experience with already. Basically, he was volunteering to go to jail of his own accord. Now, you might be wondering if the crappy food and the lack of freedom were difficult for him. Nope. First of all, he'd suffered far worse indignities than those during his time on the outside. Since the day he was born, he'd learned how to grin and bear it.

What if he got sick? He knew there were people called doctors for that sort of thing. It was their job to worry about that all the time. Still, he had some trouble with the small portions of food at the beginning, but soon he came to realize that they were plenty, considering that all he did was sit around, "play," and sleep all day. In fact, he was getting a little chubby.

As for things like the lack of freedom, that was beside the point to begin with. If you want to know why, I could push back and ask, "Well, what the hell kind of freedom did he enjoy before then?" Without getting so defensive about it, though, the real reason is because he considered being arrested by the police and going to jail to be the highest form of "freedom." If he went to jail, not only was he allowed to "play" and eat for free, he also was able to learn things. He'd have to pay for that, of course, in the form of torture and other things, but that was inevitable. Freedom, after all, is never free.

At any rate, that's how he started going back to jail. Whenever he did, his "teachers," who were bored out of their minds and had nothing better to do than to squash lice all day, were waiting for him in every cell. There were so many political prisoners and thought criminals in the police station that they couldn't separate him from them. The same was true in the prison detention center for those who were awaiting trial and those who had been convicted. No doubt even hell itself was filled to capacity in this country.

Thus, Pak Tal was taught many things in jail, but they gradually became more and more advanced. What is a state? What is an ethnic group? What are socialism and communism? What are their opposites, capitalism and imperialism? And what is war? Pak Tal listened closely to his "teachers" talk about things like world history, Korean history, the current situation in Korea, and Kim Il-sung and Syngman Rhee, asking probing questions about certain things in a low voice.

Pak Tal also first learned how to write in jail. He quickly picked up the twenty-four letters of the Korean alphabet, including vowels and consonants, learning them in about two weeks. He practiced his penmanship by scratching on the wooden floorboards, which left the index finger on his gnarled right hand worn down and the ball of his finger a little flattened.

He was taught this way by many different kinds of people. Among them were literal schoolteachers, of course, but also revolutionaries who had spent most of the past few years—from before August 15, 1945, until now—in jail or in prison. Each time he was arrested, he met new people. Pak Tal hadn't forgotten any of these people, but the one who left the deepest impression on him was a young guerrilla fighter named Kang Ch'un-min.

Before becoming a guerrilla, Kang Ch'un-min had been a student at a university in Seoul. After he joined the guerrillas, he was on a mission in the central T'aebaek Mountains, heading down to a village to contact someone, when he was captured. Finally, Pak Tal had met a genuine guerrilla for the first time in his life. Although Pak Tal didn't know it at first, Kang Ch'un-min was scheduled to be court-martialed in the near future for the sake of formality and then executed.

Unlike Pak Tal, Kang Ch'un-min was a pale young

man with a sickly air about him. During his capture, he'd been shot by a carbine, so he was still recovering from his injuries. As Pak Tal tried to care for him in various ways, he simply couldn't believe that this frail man was one of those guerrillas. But Kang Ch'un-min was a firebrand—the type you often find among young male Korean intellectuals—who talked so fast he became overbearing when he got into an argument. Once he started talking about things like ethnicity and independence, he seemed so eager to speak that the words themselves got caught in his throat, causing his head to tremble and making him blue in the face.

For that reason—and also because they were in jail where they couldn't speak as loudly as they wanted to—Kang Ch'un-min told and taught everything to Pak Tal in a hushed tone of voice. At first, Kang Ch'un-min had trouble understanding why Pak Tal would go out of his way to get arrested by the police and thrown into jail like that, so for a while he would just stare at Pak Tal's face in disbelief. Soon, though, his astonishment changed to a strong interest in Pak Tal. In that regard, Pak Tal felt the same way about him.

They were both the same age, twenty-four or twenty-five, but they were completely different people in every other respect. One was the son of an urban and somewhat bourgeois family, not to mention a university student, while the other was a poor farmer's son—and a supposedly "ignorant and uneducated" farmhand at that—who didn't even know his parents' whereabouts.

In their case, however, the fact that they were so different brought them even closer together. Kang Ch'un-min tried to hammer everything he knew—all the things he'd learned until that point—into Pak Tal's head. Indeed, sometimes he got so irritated that he came down hard on Pak Tal, much like a hammer.

He was also the person who first taught Pak Tal how to write. Strangely enough, even though the day of his execution hadn't been set, he seemed to know when it was, for as that fateful day drew closer, he started to become even more irritable. For those few days, Pak Tal continued with his studies, barely sleeping. Kang Ch'un-min was up all night as well, but for a different reason.

One of those mornings, the guard opened the iron door and summoned Kang Ch'un-min. The guard spoke in a strangely compassionate voice. In a similarly tender voice, Kang said to Pak Tal, "Thanks for everything, little buddy . . . ." Then he handed him all of his possessions (which only amounted to a few pieces of unused tissue paper and an old worn-out hand towel) and left the cell. Pak Tal stood there in stunned silence as he watched Kang Ch'un-min leave.

The period from the end of 1949 to 1950 saw the fiercest fighting against the guerrillas in southern Korea. To leave someone like Kang Ch'un-min in a police station jail—even for just a few days—was the exception rather than the norm. Under the command of the American military, the defense forces waged repeated campaigns of "subjugation." When the guerrillas were captured, they were rounded up and killed on the spot.

Needless to say, Kang Ch'un-min never came back. But Pak Tal was still alive. He was not just alive; he was learning how to read and write Korean letters. Although there were still some mistakes in his spelling and so forth, once he was able to write flyers in his own hand, he began showing signs of yet another abrupt transformation.

How did he change, you ask? Well, in a nutshell, he stopped "volunteering" to go to jail as he'd done before. He realized that even if he didn't "volunteer" to go to jail, he could go there anytime he wanted, as long as he put into practice the things he wanted to say—in other words, the things he'd learned from his "teachers" inside that jail. That wasn't the only way he changed, though. Now, when he got arrested, he was more concerned with getting out of jail as soon as possible. He quickly put this into practice as well. In other words, our hero Pak Tal, who was supposedly a vile political prisoner and thought criminal, suddenly "converted."

"Yessir! I knew it was wrong. Yessir! I will never do it again, Sir. Eh-heh-heh . . . ."

Who knows how many times he'd been arrested until then—including going to the police and turning himself in—and how many times he'd "converted" like this.

Now, dear readers, you might be wondering, *Why did this writer introduce such a ridiculous character?* However, that's not my responsibility. He's just that kind of human being, so I have no choice in the matter. This "self-awakened" Pak Tal, if you will, was the product of Kang Ch'un-min and all the other political prisoners and thought criminals in jail who each had a hand in creating him. In terms of his penchant for "conversion," however, he turned out completely different than them.

Was it possible that they taught him about such things

as "conversion"? No, of course not. Had they taught him about that, they would have taught him to do the exact opposite. Besides, there was no need to bother teaching him the greatest lesson they were demonstrating with their own bodies. And clearly Pak Tal had learned from their example.

Take Kang Ch'un-min, for example. He was the scion of an old bourgeois family back in Keijō (Seoul), so imagine what would have happened if he'd contacted his parents and asked them to pay some money to the right people to take out one of those newspaper ads (i.e., statements of conversion) that say stuff like, "I hereby pledge allegiance to His Excellency President So-and-So and to the Republic of Korea." In all likelihood, he wouldn't have been executed.

Back then, those kind of newspaper ads came out almost daily. Actually, even in Kang Ch'un-min's case, a couple of the guards urged him to recant, sticking their faces against the metal grating of the iron door every time they came by, but it was hard to tell if they were doing that out of genuine kindness or if they were trying to get something out of it. However, Kang was in the middle of doing his damnedest to teach *batchim* (a principle

114

THE TRIAL OF PAK TAL AND OTHER STORIES

of Korean spelling) to Pak Tal, so he furiously knitted his brows and yelled, "Shut the hell up!" Kang Ch'un-min was not the only one they were trying to convert. Almost everyone in that jail would have been released, at least for the time being, had they just made this kind of "conversion." But they did not. They refused to. When Pak Tal realized this, he was deeply moved.

Wow, these people are amazing! Pak Tal would think as he carefully studied the faces of the men around him again. Song Ǔl-yang and the other old men had been living in prison since the days of the Japanese occupation. Now, they were so emaciated they looked like those dried fish called *myeongtae* (pollock). They were just waiting to die.

Despite his admiration for these men, however, our hero Pak Tal chose to "convert." How the hell did this happen? Perhaps he would say it was an expression of his own individuality. If so, then he was one heck of an individual, but that doesn't tell us very much. Ultimately, he ended up setting off on his own path. It was also around this time that Pak Tal began earnestly kowtowing the minute he saw a police officer or the public prosecutor, wildly screaming when they roughed him up a little, and randomly chuckling, "Eh-heh-heh . . ."

Right before the last war began, that rascal Pak Tal took the entire town by surprise with flyers he'd written by hand, the first time he'd written anything in his life. Before then, the townspeople had written him off as nothing more than an eccentric, but thanks to this flyer incident, he became a celebrity almost overnight.

Within the country, it was starting to get somewhat chaotic. Just when it began to look like the guerrillas had finally lost their organizational strength due to repeated "subjugation" campaigns, cries of "March north for reunification" now arose out of nowhere. Meanwhile, northern Korea dispatched an envoy to negotiate a North-South unification deal, but he was arrested the moment he arrived, and the next thing you know that old man Dulles, whose face looked like a crow, came over from America to do an "inspection" of the 38th parallel. In this explosive situation, the town was quickly suffused with a suffocating atmosphere, everyone fearing that a civil war between the North and the South might break out any minute.

Flyers with slogans like "March north for reunification—sweep away the Commie bastards!" and "Onward to Mt. Paektu! Onward to the Yalu River!" were plastered about town, and people were rounded up and herded off to public speeches on such topics almost daily. If they refused to go, their food rations would be stopped. The sound of military boots marching through the streets grew louder and more intense by the day.

One day, out of the blue, a completely different type of flyer popped up all over town, catching people's eyes. People read them quickly, looking around nervously to make sure that no one was watching. The flyers said, "north or south, we're all koreans, stop fighting!" "release all the political prisoners!" and "don't listen to what japanamerica says!" They were painstakingly written in rudimentary Korean letters only—with no Chinese characters—and were posted on walls and telephone poles in alternating order throughout the town. I'm not quite sure what the word "japanamerica" was referring to, but it probably meant "America in place of Japan."

The townspeople were so surprised they could hardly believe their own eyes. The flyers were clearly the work of a leftist, so they seemed to set the entire town abuzz almost overnight. Even more surprised than the people, though, were the police and the military police, who were left literally speechless. They ran around in all directions tearing down the flyers and immediately launched a search for the formidable culprit.

But they had no idea who did it. Pak Tal, who was working in a certain blacksmith's shop in town at the time, did cross their minds, but there was no way Pak Tal could write like that, so they ruled out him out right away. If they suggested something like that to their supervisor, they might be ridiculed. They didn't have the time or the energy to investigate the fact that the letters—if you could even call them that—were terribly clumsy and the penmanship was a little funny.

No matter what, we have to catch the criminal as soon as possible. That was the only thought in their minds. So, as usual, they began going around town arresting anyone and everyone who seemed the least bit suspicious. That included people who had "converted" earlier and people they'd been keeping their eyes on for a while, but oddly enough, they completely overlooked Pak Tal.

Pak Tal was not pleased about this. The fact that both the police and the military police had ignored him wasn't what made him unhappy. Well, that's not entirely true, but what he found even more surprising and vexing was that innocent people were being arrested and tortured

THE TRIAL OF PAK TAL AND OTHER STORIES

because of what he'd done.

He'd never anticipated this. So, having no other choice, he wrote two flyers like the ones he'd put up and took them down to the police station, where he turned himself in.

"I'm the one who did it. Eh-heh-heh . . ." he said, thrusting the two flyers in the faces of the police officers.

Evidently, the police officers were so surprised they just sat there for a moment with their mouths hanging open. Again, they were speechless. Pak Tal, of course, was thrown into jail. When the townspeople found out, they thought, *He might not get off so easily this time. He might be . . .*

Just then, however, the Korean War broke out on June 25, 1950. Once the war actually began, the defense forces, despite their big talk, were crushed by the northern Korean People's Army in no time. The police station in this town quickly surrendered, releasing all of its political prisoners and thought criminals, including Pak Tal. Jumping for joy, Pak Tal was greeted by cheering crowds when he got out. The town, he discovered, had already been liberated by the Korean People's Army.

Like many people, our hero Pak Tal was not necessarily a war supporter, but he volunteered for the army twice during this conflict. The first time was for the Korean People's Army, which had come from the North.

When the Korean People's Army surged south, they found themselves fighting the American military and the United Nations Command, which had intervened on behalf of the South, so they were recruiting for a frontline volunteer army even in this area. The recruitment took place in the schoolyard of an elementary school in town. Pak Tal eagerly marched himself right on over there.

Pak Tal already knew quite a bit about northern Korea and the Korean People's Army from his indoctrination by those political prisoners and thought criminals in jail. He got excited at the very thought of finally achieving the unfinished goals of land reform and socialism here in southern Korea. *When this war is over*, he thought, *I might be able to go back to my farming village. Then I could rent two small cows and . . .*

In all his excitement, however, he made an unforeseeable blunder.

The person in charge of selecting volunteer army cadets from the large group of applicants was a young political officer about the same age as Pak Tal. This made Pak Tal so happy for some reason that he accidentally laughed out loud at the officer with his usual "Eh-heh-heh."

The officer stared at Pak Tal for some time with a dubious look on his face. Cursing to himself, Pak Tal hurriedly tried to wipe the smile off his face, but that only made his expression look even stranger. He became more and more agitated.

But the political officer said, "Comrade, please, just try to do your best at the rear," and courteously kicked him out of the courtyard. The officer in question had completely failed to recognize the socialist in Pak Tal. Then again, who wouldn't?

The second time he volunteered was for the South's national defense forces. The Korean People's Army had retreated, and the fighting was concentrated along the 38th parallel. Following behind the American military and the United Nations Command, the defense forces were finally, if hurriedly, trying to rearrange their battle lines. In addition to calling for volunteers to join them across the country, they were rounding up all the young men they could find and reorganizing their units.

Pak Tal had an idea. *If I just sit here like this*, he thought, *they're bound to find me sooner or later, so I*

might as well just go over there myself and volunteer for
their stupid army! He remembered what had happened
with the Korean People's Army, so this time he purposely
opened his mouth as wide as he could and did you-know-
what twice in a row.

"Gentlemen, thank you for your truly heroic efforts.
Eh-heh-heh . . . eh-heh-heh . . ."

Just like last time, the man who was staffing the
reception desk—a junior officer, by the looks of it—stared
at Pak Tal dubiously for a moment. Pak Tal got a little
flustered, thinking it might not work. This time, though,
his confusion seemed to have the intended effect.

"Get the hell outta here! We have no use for lunatics
like you!" the petty officer screamed and sent him away
with a swift kick in the ass.

Pak Tal scurried home, clutching his rear end
and hopping like a bunny. As for the junior officer in
question—well, he may have been surprisingly perceptive
about Pak Tal after all.

At any rate, Pak Tal was thus exempted from military
service by both sides. While the war raged on around
him, he lived a relatively peaceful life. Of course, during
this tense war, there was the constant fear of being shot to

death on the spot—no questions asked—if you made the wrong move, so he probably just wanted to stay alive. He knew how pointless it would be to die a dog's death. So, he lay low for a while, working as a night-soil man.

When the war ended, though, he sprang back into action. As he would say, he had no choice but to get back to work. In July 1953, after three years, a cease-fire agreement was finally reached. Even though the war was finally over with nothing to show for it other than scorched earth across most of the country, here in the South, people hadn't learned their lesson yet and were still shouting things like "March north for reunification."

At that point, our hero Pak Tal rose up and took matters into his own hands! While it might feel good to say something so courageous, the way he went about it was a bit unconventional. He prepared small scraps of paper, on which he carefully wrote the phrase "good work, men, now wouldya please go home." The act of writing was fun in and of itself, so he could have done it for days.

Thus, he took those leaflets and stood on the street, where he handed them out one by one to the American soldiers who passed by. Pak Tal thought the reason why

The Trial of Pak Tal

people hadn't learned anything from the war and were still shouting things like "March north for reunification—wipe out the Commie bastards" was because the American military was still there.

Here was the root of the problem. Everyone knew it was impossible to wage such a war with only the South's defense forces, judging from the way they'd run away and fallen apart at the beginning of the last war.

When the American soldiers glanced at the incomprehensible writing on the leaflets, some just tossed them aside and went on their way. When that happened, Pak Tal would chase after them, pick up the leaflet, and give it back to them. He would stuff it into their pants pocket. *How rude,* he thought, *to throw away something that someone poured their heart and soul into for so many sleepless nights!*

Among the many soldiers, there were a few courteous ones who accepted Pak Tal's leaflets with a friendly smile, some of them even sticking out their hand to shake his and saying, "Oh, thank you."

Pak Tal shook their hands vigorously, getting the feeling that these Americans really sympathized with what he was trying to say.

An old policeman came out of the alley across the street and stood there watching with a vague grin on his face.

Wondering what was going on, the kind-looking old policeman came in for a closer look. Pak Tal slunk to the side and gradually moved farther away. He wanted to get rid of all the leaflets in his hand as fast as he could. The old policeman approached him.

"Whatcha got there?" the old policeman asked, peering into Pak Tal's hand.

With a straight face, Pak Tal handed him one of the leaflets. Then he grabbed another American soldier and handed him one as well.

When he read the leaflet that Pak Tal gave him, the old policeman just stood there for a while in a daze, not saying anything. He looked on as Pak Tal handed out more leaflets. But then he began shaking furiously. He violently grabbed Pak Tal's arm and sputtered, "Uh, um." Taking a deep gulp, he finally blurted out, "You're under arrest!"

Thus, Pak Tal got arrested again. This was his first arrest since the end of the last war.

This time, however, he was released rather quickly,

either because the entire police department—from the police chief on down—had been replaced due to the war or because there were a few Korean nationalists among them who sympathized with Pak Tal's flyers. They probably concluded that Pak Tal was a madman, or something very close to it.

As usual, the jail was filled with political prisoners and thought criminals. What was different this time around was the number of former government officials who were there on suspicion of collaborating with the Korean People's Army during its invasion. In this country, the police station jails and the prisons are always up to their ears with these types of people.

Soon thereafter, Pak Tal was arrested again. For crying out loud, how many times had he been arrested since the war ended? And each time he got out of jail by pledging to convert, saying, "Yessir! I will never do it again, Sir."

Still, he showed no signs of "converting" whatsoever. Eventually, he was indicted by the Public Prosecutor's Office. Recently, even the police officers were afraid of him and rarely approached him on the street anymore. That's because, when Pak Tal was arrested in town, the police officers almost always used their standard tactics of pummeling him with their fists and their boots, except in rare cases like that of the old policeman whom I described earlier.

However, when the police officers finished punching and kicking him like that, they found leaflets in their pockets with messages like "oppose the northward advance no more wars!" and "the koreans fought the americans, but they didn't fight the soviets!" All the stuff about the Americans, of course, was referring to the most recent war.

A police officer was almost fired for this very reason when his supervisor discovered one of those leaflets somewhere on his uniform during an inspection. In this case, the officer was able to bluff his way out of it and keep his job, but thereafter, if any other police officers got anywhere near Pak Tal, they had to inspect their own uniforms right away before doing anything else.

The inspection itself was no big deal, but it took a lot of time. Those who were a little neurotic felt anxious for days, unable to relax. They even took off their underpants and shook them out, worried there might still be some leaflets tucked away in there somewhere. There was also the case of an officer who took a long time to realize that a tiny folded leaflet had been wedged behind the badge of his peaked cap.

Since learning how to write, Pak Tal stuck exclusively to these tactics of putting up flyers and handing out leaflets. He showed an almost abnormal degree of enthusiasm for making them, unable to contain his enjoyment as he painstakingly composed them one by one. Naturally, the more he wrote, the more polished they became.

He no longer got arrested for handing them out right in front of police officers, as he had been at the beginning, but if they saw him do it and arrested him, he didn't really mind. He had now learned another way to "hand" them to the police officers. These leaflets were made pretty cleverly, using cigarette paper and so forth. As he was being beaten up, sometimes by multiple police officers, he would slip one into their uniforms with his clumsy hands before the officers even noticed.

For Pak Tal's part, he probably intended to enlighten the police officers by doing that, but given the circumstances, now the officers had begun to keep their distance from him—an enlightened move, you might say. Let sleeping dogs lie, they thought. Well then, how did the top brass of the police and the public prosecutor view this troublesome "dog"? Needless to say, none of them thought very highly of him. On the contrary, they even thought of getting rid of this troublemaker on numerous occasions, just like those other "malicious" political prisoners and thought criminals.

In the case of our hero Pak Tal, though, that was easier said than done. That's because he was extremely famous in this town, albeit in a strange sort of way. By now, everyone in town had heard of him. If someone like him were to be executed, people would surely think, *Oh dear, not him!* or *Why are they so afraid of someone like Pak Tal?* Actually, the people in power were somehow afraid of how the townspeople viewed them (although their tough guy act kept them from actually recognizing it).

Moreover, Pak Tal enjoyed a certain degree of popularity not only among the townsfolk, but also— oddly enough—even inside the police station and the public prosecutor's office. The police officers and the public prosecutor in charge of dealing with him when he got arrested were sick and tired of seeing him so often, but some of the other officials smiled to themselves and even seemed to enjoy seeing him. They got a kick out of teasing and taunting him on the side, when no one was looking.

This was another reason why it was harder to get rid of him than it seemed. Instead of killing him, though, the police officers and the public prosecutor in charge of the case used torture and punishment techniques on him that were utterly barbaric. Whether or not that was a good thing is impossible to say, but Pak Tal now knew all their dirty little tricks, so he was able to keep them down to a bare minimum.

More precisely, because Pak Tal was already so buddy-buddy with them, he even derived a kind of pleasure—a sense of purpose—from fighting with an enemy whose strengths and weaknesses he knew inside and out. To put it another way, it would not be such an exaggeration to say that he made regular visits to the jail and the detention center for that very purpose. When these two adversaries met, their "struggle" was really something to behold . . . . Those of you, dear readers, who are familiar with fiction might be thinking, *We've had enough of your narrative asides. Why don't you just show us the scene already?*

There's no need to worry about that, though. I shall describe this for you in great detail soon, the next time Pak Tal is arrested. He will definitely be arrested again—

there's no doubt about that. Here, let me add just one more thing: how, then, was he seen by the underground organization of the Workers' Party, which also existed in this town? This question is a bit tricky for me. Actually, I know very little about that aspect of society, but it's not so hard to guess. In a word, although they sometimes were amazed by Pak Tal's sheer audacity, for the most part they kept their distance from him, in the literal sense of respecting him from afar. No wonder. After all, what use could they possibly have for a man who slavishly kowtowed to the police officers and the public prosecutor as soon as he was arrested and promised to "convert" each time?

It feels a little odd to say this, but there are just some things you have to accept. As for the fundamental problem of our hero Pak Tal's "integrity," he himself was often criticized by his "teachers" in the jail and the detention center. They even tried knocking some sense into him about it.

Every time, though, he just replied, "Yessir . . . You have your way, and that's fine. And I have my way, and that's fine too." He also said, "At any rate, I can't do anything if I'm in here all the time. I don't wanna waste my time like this. Plus, I'm a peasant by nature. I've always been that way, and I always will be." He didn't say another word.

It's about time for me to stop talking about Pak Tal's past and get on with the story, but while we're at it, how did Pak Tal end up together with Tan-sŏn, who has just put him to bed in her room and is now boiling water? It's quite simple, really. He came to live with this woman named Tan-sŏn after his first introduction to a detention center a little while ago.

Until then, Pak Tal had been working as a kind of manservant in the local bar where Tan-sŏn now worked as a cook. It may not have looked like it from the outside, but the bar was making and distributing a fair amount of moonshine, so they needed a man like him—especially one like him—to help out.

In other words, this bar occasionally got raided by the police, either because they'd neglected to bribe the police or—if they had bribed them—because they'd given bribes to some officers and not others (in reality, it's hard to go around bribing everyone equally). At times like this, it was very helpful to have a man like Pak Tal around who didn't mind getting taken into custody by the police. The proprietress had hired him specifically with that in mind.

Before they were raided, though, Pak Tal ended up getting arrested through circumstances of his own making—or, as the proprietress would say, due to that "sickness" of his. He was arrested for handing out those leaflets and slipping them into police officers' pockets again. How on earth he'd made them in such short order was anybody's guess. Thus, he was sent to the detention center for the first time and finally got out about three months later, when the charges were dropped.

Pak Tal came back to the bar where he used to work. The way he came back was also typical of him. As usual, he went around town delivering messages from his cellmates to various people. It was after dark by the time he finally arrived, but he came right in like someone who had just stepped out for a moment. Without saying a word, he immediately grabbed a broom and started sweeping the floor and cleaning up the bowls of *t'akchu* the customers had left scattered on the tables. For his part, he seemed to be trying to get caught up with his work all at once after being away for three months.

When the proprietress spotted him, however, her

eyeballs almost popped out of her head. Her house had been searched by the police after he was arrested. She ran over to him and snatched a bowl right out of his hand. She pounded her hands against his chest.

"Oh my god, I could kill you! I could kill you, you little cocksucker! Do you have any idea what I went through because of you? I've had it with you! Get outta here right now. Go on, get out! Go somewhere else and fight for socialism or reunification or whatever the hell it is you want. Until that happens, I don't want to see your face again," she said, shoving him out the door. She went back inside and slammed the squeaky door shut behind her.

After being thrown out, Pak Tal was in a bit of a quandary. He had nowhere to go for the time being. Just then, the cook Tan-sǒn came around from the back door and approached him with a bashful grin on her face.

"You can go to my rented room," she said. Pak Tal slowly looked back at her dark face, which reflected her tough life: after leaving her home in the countryside, she'd been tricked into prostitution and eventually sold to a brothel in Masan.

"I thought this might happen, so I rented a room just in case. Go there and wait for me. I'll try to come home early tonight," Tan-sŏn continued, as though she'd explain everything later. Then she suddenly turned her face to the side. Maybe she was embarrassed, shall we say, to invite a man over to her place. She was not a beauty by any means, but she had a beautiful heart.

Here, dear readers, I'd like to tell you a little more about the life of this woman named Tan-sŏn, but I imagine you must be tired of hearing such stories about the characters' pasts, so I won't bore you with another one. Instead, I'll leave it up to your active imaginations, but if I may add just one more thing: my beloved southern Korea is full of women of this sort right now (and not just now). Some of you might be getting ready to stand up, thinking, *Well then, I'm gonna go over to Korea to get me one of those women for myself,* but I'd politely recommend against it.

Here's why: not only is it hard to go to southern Korea on the spur of the moment right now, but women like that also have an extremely strong sense of ethnic pride and class consciousness. They acquired this from their own experiences, and when you see what Tan-sŏn does from now on, you'll understand just how strong these women are. Bourgeois types and foreigners—especially Japanese and Americans—don't stand a chance with them. The only person who can win the heart of a woman like this is a man like our hero Pak Tal.

So how did Pak Tal respond to her advances? As you know, he had plenty of experience with being taken into police custody, but he still had no experience with marriage. I'm not very knowledgeable about private matters like that, but I imagine he'd never been with a woman before. In other words, being a complete *ch'onggak* (bachelor), he naturally got flustered by Tan-sŏn's affections and could barely keep his heart from beating out of his chest.

These were the circumstances through which our hero Pak Tal came to live with Tan-sŏn. Well now, it appears that Tan-sŏn has finished boiling the water. As before, Pak Tal was lying on his back and staring at the ceiling, his big body sprawled out on the floor. There were no traces of the tears in his eyes from a moment ago.

Not only were his tears gone, but his eyes were also shining vividly, even giving off a strange light. What could he be thinking about? In the darkness, the glint in his eyes made them appear to be ablaze with vengeance. If Public Prosecutor for Law and Order Kim Nam-ch'ŏl, who was in charge of his case, could see this light in his eyes right now, he would surely gasp in surprise . . . .

Before long, Tan-sŏn came into the room with a washtub of hot water. She took off all of Pak Tal's clothes, stripping him to the skin. Then she carefully began wiping his body using two towels in turn. Pak Tal's body, which was filthy from the past few months in the detention center, looked as if it were covered in a layer of dirt, and the two towels quickly turned black. She also changed the water in the tub multiple times.

Perhaps pretending to be a handsome man, Pak Tal stood there with his shoulders squared, letting her do as she pleased. When the layer of grime had finally been scraped off, the original surface of his fairly white skin appeared. Now, though, Tan-sŏn saw that his entire body was covered in cuts and bruises. Scars from the leather belts used on him during repeated torture sessions zigzagged across his body. Even in the darkness, they clearly stood out, like black strokes of ink on white paper.

Tan-sŏn grimaced for a moment, as though it pierced her heart to see this, but she continued wiping him down without saying a word. Soon, when she got to his groin, she let out a little giggle. Pak Tal also twisted his body and laughed. Hmmm . . . Apparently, a natural physiological phenomenon had occurred.

When she finished wiping off the area around his buttocks, she stood up and started laying out the bedding on the floor. She took out a stiffly starched sheet and spread it out on the mattress. Holding Pak Tal in her arms, she laid him down on the bed. Then she went outside again. This time, she began washing Pak Tal's dirty clothes with the leftover bathwater. She was a very hard-working woman.

When it seemed like she was finally done, she took off her robe and lay down next to Pak Tal, who whispered sweet nothings to her like "Ahh" and whatnot. Lying on their backs, the two were strangely silent for a while.

"What about next time . . . ?" Tan-sŏn asked, giggling about something she'd remembered. "What are you planning to do next time?"

"Hmm, good question. Next time will be a strike! We're gonna hit those guys hard and knock 'em off their feet. But we need a union for that. First, we gotta form a union," Pak Tal replied.

He had seemed sheepish when Tan-sŏn crawled under the covers, but now his voice was suddenly alive.

"You made up your mind when you met that guy Mr. Ch'oe earlier, didn't you? I kind of saw you talking to him. If you and Mr. Ch'oe worked together, I think you could pull it off."

"Hmm."

"Is there anything I can do next time? I'll join you!"

"That's the spirit! Wow, you have changed," Pak Tal said, his voice filled with pleasure. He rolled over toward her, fiercely hugging her against his big chest. "I was worried you'd gone off and left me."

"Ah, ah . . ." she moaned. Apparently, she wanted to say, "Don't be silly," but she couldn't speak. Pak Tal moved his legs and hugged her even more tightly with both arms. You might be worrying, *What if she gets crushed by him, by his big body?* That's none of your business!

Three months went by. During the dog days of summer, when National Liberation Day, August 15, was just around the corner, the workers here in K City held a strike that looked a bit odd, at least at first glance. The term "workers" now referred only to the laborers who worked on the American military base; there was nowhere else to work in town. One day, they all walked

The Trial of Pak Tal

off the job in unison.

"In unison," though, didn't mean every single one of them. They tried to present a united front, but it didn't quite work out that way. A few of the aircraft maintenance crew—the mechanics, for short—and some other people, including a bunch of guys known as interpreters, didn't participate. The organizers did their best to persuade them otherwise, but they never came around to the idea, some of them laughing if off and others making a long face. Of course, these fellows showed no interest in joining the union, either.

As a result, Ch'oe Tong-kil and Pak Tal were not able to "knock 'em off their feet," as they'd planned, but almost all the other miscellaneous workers—who were divided into various categories collectively known as "labor"—participated in the strike. K Base was a relatively small base for South Korea, and there were only about 400 Koreans working there. But when more than half of them joined the strike, operations inside the base all but ground to a halt.

As for the small number of mechanics and others who didn't participate, it wasn't as if they worked independently of the other workers, so naturally the base fell into a state of paralysis. These workers were also on edge, anxious about their own jobs.

To make matters worse, the strike happened suddenly, with no notification, turning the base into a ghost town. The work areas that had been filled with groups of workers until the day before suddenly looked vacant. Now they just sat empty and exposed to the harsh light of the midsummer sun. Ants swarmed on the handle of a shovel somebody had left out.

As for the town, it was also quiet as a mouse that day because the workers were all holed up in their separate homes, awaiting word from someone and ruminating on various matters. They weren't alone, though. Even their families stayed inside, watching and waiting to see what would happen.

Throughout the world, when people hear the word "strike," they think of demonstrations and placards, but here in my beloved southern Korea, those are a thing of the past. If they did stuff like that here, the military would be dispatched, and the strikers would be suppressed in no time. That was another reason why Pak Tal and the others had so much trouble organizing the strike.

To begin with, before they could even go on strike,

they had to go through a long process of painstaking efforts and heated arguments. First, they began by forming a labor union, as planned. That was relatively easy to accomplish. Of course, everything was carried out in secret, but one factor behind their early success was the decision to mobilize the widely popular mechanic named Chŏn Sang-t'aek from the very beginning, as Ch'oe Tong-kil had recommended.

Chŏn Sang-t'aek used to be a soldier in the defense forces or something like that, so he was one of the younger mechanics on the base. Oddly enough, though, everyone looked up to him. He appeared to just keep his head down and do his job day in and day out, but there was something intellectual about him. Furthermore, even though he was already about thirty-four or thirty-five, he was still single and lived alone, renting a room in Old Man Cho Sŏk-u's house. Perhaps for that reason, some people secretly suspected that he was a member of the underground Workers' Party. No one would say that out loud, however.

Perhaps because they knew Chŏn Sang-t'aek was leading the strike, the workers mostly thought, *If everyone's joining the strike, then so will I.* This attitude probably came from that spirit of solidarity behind adages like "There's safety in numbers" or "If we're all going to die, we might as well die together." Plus, it goes without saying that Pak Tal ran around trying to persuade them by offering to go to the police and get arrested anytime they needed him to. Still, even though they had a union, none of them believed for a moment that it would be allowed to function legally.

They acted out of a sense of despair. They wanted something—anything, really—that would somehow shatter the status quo. This gave them the courage to form a union. After going around and discussing it with Pak Tal and the others, they made Chŏn Sang-t'aek the chairman. For the vice-chairman, they chose the so-called intellectual Ri Chŏng-chu, who finally caved in after everyone pushed him to do it. That dashing young man Ch'oe Tong-kil became the secretary-general. Pak Tal became a committee member.

Thus, with the three key positions filled and the committee members chosen, the union was finally ready. The funny thing is (though it's not a laughing matter at all), they then faced a big question. Chŏn Sang-t'aek and the others probably realized this from the start, even if they didn't talk about it, but how would they get the base authorities and the police to recognize them as a union? To put it another way, they had to decide who would notify the authorities and how, like the mice in the fable "Belling the Cat."

Pak Tal raised his hand, but he was quickly turned down. They needed someone whose talents went beyond simply not being afraid of getting caught by the police. The next person to volunteer was "dog guard" Chŏn Man-sŏk. He argued for going on strike immediately. In other words, he was the first person to support the strike.

"Once we show up and tell them what we've done, they'll bust the union for sure. If we can take them by surprise even for just a day, then that's still a victory for us. That was my plan from the very beginning," Chŏn Man-sŏk said, squinting his sharp eyes. Secretary-General Ch'oe Tong-kil agreed with him immediately.

Actually, Ch'oe had been itching to say the same thing himself for some time. As you dear readers will recall from a short while ago, he was the one who was itching to go on strike and who had "that plan from the very beginning."

Then Pak Tal said, "Hmm, I agree," nodding his head

with a serious look on his face. After a while (since Ch'oe spoke up during that time), he turned to Chŏn Man-sŏk and gave a low nod one more time, as if to show how much he admired Chŏn's opinion.

However, Pak Tal didn't say another word. Now that they had a union and had come this far in their deliberations, he knew what his role was, so he kept that to himself and remained silent.

Nonetheless, things proceeded along the lines of Chŏn Man-sŏk's argument. Chŏn Man-sŏk was a man who had won everyone's trust in a slightly strange way, albeit differently than Chŏn Sang-t'aek, mainly because of the following episode.

Chŏn Man-sŏk was one of the "dog guards," night watchmen who guarded the base accompanied by trained dogs. In addition, there were supervisors who watched over them. American officers were assigned this duty, and pairs of them would go around from time to time to check on him and the other guards.

One rainy night, after many weeks of planning, Chŏn Man-sŏk let his dog loose on the officers in the dark. It was hilarious. The drunken officers grabbed their guns from their holsters and fired blindly at the dog as they hightailed it out of there.

The next day, this quickly became a scandal, but Chŏn Man-sŏk was actually praised by Lieutenant Colonel Kirk, the commanding officer of the base, for his "loyal service." Rumor had it that the commanding officer himself was afraid of Chŏn Man-sŏk, who had a sharp eye—like an eagle—for taming and controlling highly trained dogs. At any rate, the workers knew what had really happened.

Now, those workers were about to rush headlong into a strike.

"Well then, I guess this means we're going on strike to demand recognition of our union. But . . . is that our only demand? Aren't there other things we want to ask for?" Chairman Chŏn Sang-t'aek asked.

"Of course. But first we need to make those guys recognize us as a union. Then we can deal with the other stuff."

"Yeah, that's the first priority. Our demands should come after that. We've got plenty of things to ask for!"

Chŏn Man-sŏk and a few others said these things at the same time. Indeed, they had a laundry list of demands. First and foremost was the issue of their terribly low wages, which never went up—as opposed to prices, which went up by the day for some reason—even if you "worked your tongue off" (which is also why they could "easily" go on strike and take a day "off" from work). And then there was the issue of their own semi-independent country, which was causing this to happen....

Although this was a much larger issue concerning the ethnic and political problems of reunification and independence, Chŏn Sang-t'aek's words elicited a series of clamorous opinions on those things as well. If I were to write them down here, they would go something like this.

"Grilled or boiled, our country tastes best when we cook it ourselves, so it's time for you guys to get outta the kitchen and go home. That's what we should tell 'em."

"And this, too. Communist or not, the North doesn't scare folks like us one little bit. In the last war, they turned out to be Koreans just like us!"

Here, people burst out laughing in spite of themselves. Then someone said, "Shh!"

"Either one is fine. We should just draw straws to pick a side and then get together and become independent...."

"Yeah, take that old geezer with you and get the hell outta Korea!"

The Trial of Pak Tal

And so on. This time, too, though, Pak Tal just sat there smiling to himself without saying a word.

That's because he'd already finished making flyers that said pretty much the same things. The flyers were buried beside a certain street, deep beneath a rock he used to mark the exact spot.

Chŏn Sang-t'aek, however, was well aware of these things, except for Pak Tal's flyers. I don't know if he was a member of the underground Workers' Party or not, but I must say that he didn't seem too enthusiastic about this hasty strike. *Don't we have any other options?* he wondered.

But what other choice did they have?!

Even if they tried to pursue peaceful negotiations, once they showed up and told the authorities what they'd done, the union would be busted in no time, just like Chŏn Man-sŏk had said. Of course, there would also be casualties.

In other words, Chŏn Sang-t'aek was forced to go with the flow. The tactics they used afterward, though, were mostly his ideas. Once he resolved to go ahead with the strike, he even thought for a moment, *If it's just a matter of making them recognize the formation of the union,*

THE TRIAL OF PAK TAL AND OTHER STORIES

there's a chance we might succeed. He had good reason to believe that.

After all, labor unions were not entirely unheard of, even here in North and South Korea. The basis for his thinking was: since there were unions—company unions, but unions nonetheless—then maybe they would recognize ours. Whether or not it would turn out that way, however, was a different question. What happened next will reveal the answer to that.

By late morning, the base authorities finally caught on to this "organized shutdown" and quickly began to panic. They called the Labor Procurement Management Office and the police station at the same time and chewed them out. They sped around in jeeps. They were pretty much "knocked off their feet." *Not these goddamn Koreans again,* they thought. Was it a revolution? A rebellion? The fact that the town was quiet as a mouse was actually rather eerie.

The director of the Labor Procurement Management Office, who was rubber-stamping documents with an annoyed look on his face—still unable to forget his failed attempt to sleep with a *kisaeng* (female entertainer) who

had caught his eye at a drinking party the night before—
was particularly caught off guard. He was so surprised, in
fact, that he jumped to his feet and quickly switched on
the radio, thinking the North Korean People's Army had
launched another attack. The radio was playing a popular
song sung in a tearful, plaintive tone.

Officials from the Labor Procurement Management
Office fanned out in all directions. They joined forces
with the police officers and rushed into a nearby worker's
house.

"Wh-what the hell are you guys doing? Why aren't you
at work today?"

"Come again?"

Chang Tŏk-sŏng, who was fixing the stove in his
kitchen, slowly came out from the back with an innocent
look on his face, pushing his anxious-looking wife behind
him.

"I said, why aren't you at work today?"

"Oh, today's my day off . . . ."

"That's why I'm asking you: why do you have the day
off?"

"Yessir. Everybody has today off. Am I wrong?"

The next place they went, it was the same thing.

And the next, and the next after that . . . Everyone was following the rules and obeying the regulations, just like they were supposed to.

"Oh, really now? But I heard that everybody had today off. Is that not true?"

"Who told you today was a day off?"

"Maybe I heard it wrong."

"That's what I'm asking you: who told you that?"

"Well, they did say something about forming a union, and that today was—"

"What? A union? Wh-when did that happen? So you guys are members of that labor union?!"

When they heard the word "union," the officials started quaking in their boots. That's because labor unions were taboo in this region. Lieutenant Colonel Kirk, the base commander who had been transferred here from Japan, loathed unions—even company unions—so he'd given strict orders forbidding unions of any kind.

Yun T'ae-yŏng, the worker who'd mentioned the union, however, kept his cool. The fact that he hadn't mentioned it until that point was all part of the plan.

"If everyone's a member, I guess I am too. But I'm still really confused about the whole thing. First of all, unions and whatnot have been strictly forbidden here for many years . . . . Who in the world would come up with such a crazy idea? Don't you fellas know?"

"Of course not! How the hell are we supposed to know? Now tell us, who formed the union?"

"I see. I just assumed that you fellas ordered us to do it. I see . . . . Well, if that's the case, I'd better go tell everyone right away."

At each place, they went through the same rigamarole. Everywhere they went, the answer was always the same: "Well, I'll be damned! You mean to tell me that today wasn't a day off?"

After being dragged out of their homes by the officials, the workers, including some women, slowly streamed toward the main plaza inside the base. When they converged on the entrance of the base from all three directions, they exchanged smiles and waved to each other.

Everything was proceeding according to plan. The way they assembled like that at the base, after being dragged out of their homes by the officials, was all part of the plan. Even the way Yun T'ae-yŏng told the officials about the union had gone as planned. Whether or not their plan would ultimately succeed, however, was another matter. For instance, what if they'd told the officials and the police about the union in advance?

By the time they'd finished gathering in the plaza in front of the base's administration building, it was exactly noon. Once they saw the others assemble like this, those who hadn't participated in the strike that day wondered what on earth was going on and naturally came out to join them. Contrary to expectation—although this, too, was planned—it turned into a huge demonstration. At last, it was time to begin collective bargaining.

Just then, however, truckloads of police and American soldiers bearing carbines rushed into the plaza one after another, completely encircling the workers in no time. Those who hadn't participated in the strike frantically tried to slip away, but they were driven back by the American soldiers' bayonets.

The police forces, which included backup from a nearby station, and the American soldiers, who seemed to comprise an entire squadron, were fully armed. Some of them were even setting up heavy machine guns on the far side of the plaza. Then, with a deafening rumble, three tanks arrived, barreling straight into the crowd. As soon as the tanks arrived, they started spinning around in circles, wriggling their gun turrets like elephant trunks.

Wearing caps fastened with chin straps, the chief of police and the director of the Labor Procurement Management Office tumbled out of their jeep, sweat dripping down their faces. Next, Lieutenant Colonel Kirk, the base commander, arrived in a motorcade. The authorities lined up in front of the administration building and faced the workers, who were now surrounded on all sides. The commander, standing in the middle, was accompanied by a bodyguard: an American soldier carrying a machine gun. They stood there like that for a while, trying to pick out the "instigators"—which is to say the union leaders—from among the workers.

The workers were getting antsy. The demonstration they'd planned had now turned into the perfect chance for their enemies to surround and capture them. The union leaders, who stood near the middle, had turned pale, including the normally fervent Chŏn Sang-t'aek. He'd prepared himself for this kind of crackdown sooner or later. However, he always thought they would target him and a few other leaders; he never intended to drag everyone else into it like this.

Ri Chŏng-chu and the others were trembling with cowardice. The only one who was his usual energetic self (even if he was just putting on a brave face) was Secretary-General Ch'oe Tong-kil. Nevertheless, they began conferring with each other, eager to begin bargaining as quickly as possible.

Just then, Pak Tal, looking straight ahead, stepped out from behind them and said, "That's all for today, men. I'll take it from here. Just sit tight and stay put. And hold down the fort while I'm gone."

Then Pak Tal moved forward, pushing his way through the crowd. His words—which he uttered in a low voice that seemed to force its way up from deep in his belly—were filled with such dignified determination that Ri Chŏng-chu's legs suddenly stopped shaking. He looked back at Pak Tal's face in disbelief.

Pak Tal continued straight ahead. When the agitated workers saw him, they fell silent, momentarily lost for words. Under the blazing midsummer sun, everything seemed to stop—including the people they were facing off against—like a scene from a film frozen in time. In the frame, only Pak Tal was moving. And the people who were clearing a path for him one after another . . .

Pak Tal marched right up to the base commander, Lieutenant Colonel Kirk, and stood before him. The bodyguard thrust his machine gun at Pak Tal, but Pak Tal just grinned and gently waved it away with his hand as though he were brushing aside one of those curtains you see at entrances to shops and restaurants.

"Eh-heh-heh . . . Thank you for coming all the way out here on such a hot day, Sir," he said to the commander. He spoke in Korean of course. Lieutenant Colonel Kirk turned to the interpreter standing beside him, but before the interpreter could translate what Pak Tal had said, the chief of police and the director of the Labor Procurement Management Office jumped in from the side, nearly falling over each other.

"How dare you! Who the hell do you think you are?"

They both knew who Pak Tal was. What really pissed them off was how that lunatic Pak Tal had spoken directly to the commander, completely sidestepping them.

"Well, gentlemen, thank you for taking the time as well. I didn't mean to cause you gentlemen so much trouble today. It's just that we recently formed a union, so I had a few things to say to the commander here. Eh-heh-heh . . ."

"What?! What do you mean by a union?" the chief and the director yelled at the same time, quickly checking the expression on the commander's face. When they turned to look at each other, they nearly bumped their heads together. Their faces were twisted with undisguised hatred of each other, as if they were blaming their opponent for everything that had happened and claiming sole responsibility for dealing with the situation.

"Well, I mean a union," said Pak Tal in a loud voice.

"Then what the hell are you?"

"So what's your role in it?"

The chief and the director butted heads again.

"I'm the person in charge, so—"

"The person in charge? You mean to tell me that you're in charge of all this?" the chief of police yelled, raising a hand in disbelief and pointing at the crowd of workers standing in front of them. The workers held their breath, not saying a word as they watched the men go at it.

"Why, yes," Pak Tal answered.

"If you're the person in charge, then who's the chairman of the union?" yelled the director of the Labor Procurement Management Office this time.

"What about the vice-chairman? And the secretary-general?" the chief yelled, as if shouting at the director to quit being such a copycat.

"I am," Pak Tal replied.

The chief gave him a sharp slap across the face.

"I'm not talking about you, idiot. I'm asking who the chairman of the union is."

"I am," Pak Tal said again calmly, still reeling from the blow but steadying himself.

"What about the vice-chairman? And the secretary-general?"

"I am."

"And the secretary-general?"

"I am."

"Well, what about the other leaders?"

"I am. Eh-heh-heh . . . Chief, I'm all of them," Pak Tal said, laughing out loud.

The chief of police leapt at him, striking him on the cheekbone. Like a scarecrow, Pak Tal tumbled to the ground in an exaggerated manner. A patrolman jumped on Pak Tal and handcuffed him.

Then the chief briskly marched over to the commander and gave him a military salute, bending his back slightly. The interpreter mumbled something to the commander.

Lieutenant Colonel Kirk nodded and went inside the administration building.

After seeing the commander off, the chief raised his hand and gave the signal.

"Attack!"

The police forces surrounding the workers rushed in at once, brandishing their gunstocks. After that, it was pure pandemonium. The workers scattered in all directions, keeping low to the ground and running into each other as they tried to escape. Meanwhile, the American soldiers guarding the perimeter—even the ones who were just sitting there chewing gum—pointed their guns at any workers who came their way, raising their feet and kicking the workers back inside.

Apart from the American soldiers, the guys who belonged to the police forces were Koreans, just like the workers. If you looked at them individually, they weren't entirely bad. Actually, even when it came to this sudden attack, some of them hung back for a while, focused only on avoiding the front as much as possible by randomly walking around at the rear. Why, though, did they become so brutal as soon as they began acting as a group? Once they joined forces like this, they seemed to get intoxicated on their own power and use their own actions to fuel feelings of hatred.

Once the workers took mass action, such as going on strike, they resembled the police forces in some respects, except for using their own actions to fuel feelings of hatred. Thus, you might say they were even, at least until that point, but the workers barely put up any resistance. The police forces hit them with their gunstocks as much as they could, kicked them as much as they could, and arrested every last one of them in less than thirty minutes. Then, roped together like a chain gang, they were dragged off to the police station and the prison.

The day after the workers were all taken into custody, though, another incident shook up the town. Someone had plastered shocking flyers all over the place. They read:

"we're tired of being colonized! america, leave poor korea alone and go home! K LABOR UNION"

"communism, or anything else, is better than living under foreigners and their puppets! K LABOR UNION"

"return korea to koreans! america go home! K LABOR UNION"

As usual, the phrases on the flyers could hardly be

called "good writing," but they quickly brought the deathly silent town back to life after the incident from the day before. The flyers were posted at carefully calibrated intervals on walls and telephone poles throughout town, so there was no way not to see them, whether you wanted to or not.

Moreover, they appeared overnight, taking everyone by surprise. The police officers on night patrol had completely let down their guard, getting drunk on liquor offered to them as a reward for their daytime activities (some, no doubt, also drowned their sorrows in liquor). Thus, no one discovered the flyers during the night.

All three versions of the flyers were handwritten, not printed, with each page carefully written by brush. The characters "K LABOR UNION" caught people's eyes even more so than the main text, not only because they were so big but also because they were the only part written in Chinese characters. Clearly, someone had written them that way on purpose: to show off the existence of the union itself. Or, depending on your interpretation, they could also be taken to mean "We will never be busted, no matter what you do to us."

Huffing and puffing under the blazing sun that beat

down mercilessly on the town for yet another day, the police officers walked around taking down the flyers. People pretended not to notice.

When the chief of police first learned of the flyers, he literally jumped out of his chair in surprise.

Didn't we just arrest everyone in that "K Labor Union" yesterday? If so, maybe it was those patrolmen who arrested them and were supposed to be keeping an eye on them. If that's the case, they'll pay for this!

Or so he thought. But there was nothing in particular to suggest that.

The phone started ringing off the hook again from base headquarters, jeeps rushed over, and an emergency meeting was convened between the American military authorities and the Public Prosecutor's Office. After analyzing the handwriting on the flyers, they finally realized that it was exactly the same as Pak Tal's.

Pak Tal, however, had been arrested the day before, along with everyone else. Moreover, they'd handcuffed him before throwing him and the other leaders of the union into a strictly guarded detention center. Just to be sure, they immediately sent a patrolman over to check, but Pak Tal was still there, just as they'd thought. Then who put up those flyers, for heaven's sake?

At that point, these people, who thought only in terms of violence, finally realized that Pak Tal had a wife named Tan-sŏn. *It's gotta be her,* they thought, and drove a truck over to her place. Tan-sŏn was sitting properly in her house waiting for them to come, her black eyes gleaming. They arrested her and, while they were at it, dragged out five or six other ladies who lived in the neighborhood.

When Public Prosecutor for Law and Order Kim Nam-ch'ŏl of the K Branch Office of the M District Public Prosecutor's Office finished scrubbing his face in the morning, he went into the living room and began flipping through the paper. It was a newspaper from Seoul, printed on coarse newsprint.

While he was reading the paper, his wife would place his breakfast tray in front of him. When he was done, he'd leave for work with a solemn send-off from the members of his household, who would finally breathe a sigh of relief when he was gone. This was how he began his daily routine, but this morning he refused to take his eyes off the newspaper for some reason, even after his breakfast tray was delivered to him.

His ever-patient wife sat still, waiting for him to look up . . . . Just because he had his nose in the paper, though, didn't mean he was closely reading an article on some kind of important issue, such as the withdrawal of American troops from South Korea. Not that this was unimportant to him, mind you.

Rather, another article was of more interest to him right now than the withdrawal of American troops. His sharp gaze was focused on the bottom row of the newspaper, right above an ad for an OB/GYN clinic. There, under the heading "Judiciary Appointments," was the following four-line article:

- Public Prosecutor Chŏng Chin-ung
  H District Court Assistant Public Prosecutor
- Public Prosecutor Yun Po-ch'ul
  Appointed Judge

His eyes were glued to the page for a while, but suddenly he remembered Pak Tal and was seized with intense anger. *Dammit,* he thought, *it's all because of him I've been stuck in this branch office out in the middle of nowhere for so long. That fucking little imp! If it weren't for him, I'd be . . .* Kim Nam-ch'ŏl threw the paper aside and quickly turned to his breakfast tray. Even though he ordered his entire household—including his wife and maid—to send him off every morning with a bow, this morning he forgot to bow back. Instead, he snatched his briefcase from his wife's hands and rushed off to the Public Prosecutor's Office. *Bring it on!* he thought, gnashing his teeth.

Still, I can't believe what he did, he thought again as he quickly walked to work. *That chief judge is a useless old fart. I filed the charges and even wrote the indictment myself, but what does he do? He goes and gives the guy a suspended sentence! I'd never prosecute somebody so arbitrarily.*

Just as the Public Prosecutor's Branch Office in this city consisted of four people—the chief public prosecutor in charge of the branch office, two public prosecutors, and one clerk—the Local Branch of the District Court generally consisted of four people: the chief judge in charge of the judicial branch, two judges, and one clerk. Yu Yong-dŏk, the chief judge in this court, had a reputation for being "lenient," although he'd been on the bench since the Japanese colonial period.

When August 15, 1945, rolled around, Yu Yong-dŏk

was not yet fifty years old, but his hair went completely white almost overnight, as if marking the end of an era. For the first time in his life, he was filled with a deep sense of doubt.

Up until that point, he'd handled a number of court cases based on Japan's Peace Preservation Law. During the Pacific War in particular, he'd acted as a proxy for Japanese judges, sentencing many people to prison for many years with his own mouth. In one case, he'd even sentenced someone to death. But all of these were mistakes. In short, he'd become someone who had no idea what "the law" meant anymore. There was no doubt that the people he'd once regarded as unforgivably heinous criminals were now being treated as heroes, or at least were considered far more patriotic than he was.

His Japanese colleagues had all been repatriated, so they had nothing to worry about, but things weren't so easy for Koreans like him. For a time, Yu Yong-dŏk even thought about becoming a monk and hiding away in some mountain temple. But then the Americans came and set up the Republic of Korea, which left the Japanese judicial system in place, so he was brought back as a judge. The former Japanese Peace Preservation Law was still alive, although now it was called the National Security Act.

Thus, although Yu Yong-dŏk had no choice but to obey the law quietly, he still harbored some skepticism toward it. That's because once the political order supporting it was toppled, the law would be overturned again. This was just a fact of life, at least as far as political prisoners and thought criminals were concerned.

He had learned this from experience during the last war. When the People's Army came down from the North, the law was overturned again. You certainly didn't have to wait for the People's Army to show up to realize this. The Korean Peninsula was now clearly divided into two political orders: those who deserved the death penalty in one regime were seen as heroes in the other.

What did "the law" even mean anymore?

Thus, Yu Yong-dŏk completely lost his nerve. When it came to cases involving political prisoners and thought criminals in particular, he would blanch even more than the defendants, unsure of whose side to take. As a result, he had no choice but to become "lenient," although in this country true political prisoners and thought criminals would never be sent to courtrooms like his.

If they were brought to trial at all, it would be through what was called an expedited military tribunal. Sometimes Yu Yong-dŏk was allowed to try minor political prisoners and thought criminals from the town, such as Pak Tal, but these trials were just for show. In other words, they were for crimes of Class C and below, but they were also what allowed people like him to stay on the bench for so long.

Public Prosecutor for Law and Order Kim Nam-ch'ŏl, on the other hand, who just strode briskly through the front gate of the Public Prosecutor's Branch Office, was the polar opposite of Yu Yong-dŏk. He was still young, only thirty-six or thirty-seven years old, but he'd been a court clerk during the Japanese colonial period, so he was a man who had worked his way up from the bottom, you might say. Moreover, the anti-communist education of the time had ingrained in him a belief that there could be no independence (or anything else for that matter) until things like socialism and communism were eradicated from the face of the earth.

For Kim Nam-ch'ŏl, independence meant that each and every individual was "free" to exercise their abilities and get ahead in life according to the principle of survival of the fittest. Looking back on his own life until that point, he believed that independence was the only thing—and everything—that made our lives as human beings worth living.

Had it still been the Japanese colonial period, he could never have dreamed of being appointed a public prosecutor because even though he'd graduated from M University in Tokyo, he'd failed the Higher Civil Service Examination. He owed his career to Korea's independence after August 15, 1945. Independence was a good thing. And the biggest obstacle to independence was communism, or so he firmly believed. Therefore, he reasoned, communism also hindered his ability to get ahead in life. In a manner of speaking, this country called the Republic of Korea was the best thing that had ever happened to him. His only worry, which he kept secret, was that he suffered from epilepsy, but once he was promoted to the District Court, he was hoping to take some time off to receive treatment in America.

Unfortunately, Kim Nam-ch'ŏl had been out of town when the recent labor union incident took place. He'd left the branch office to go on a business trip to H City, where the District Court was located. Officially, he was there to

The Trial of Pak Tal

attend a meeting, but actually the main purpose of his trip was to bring a gift and pay an evening visit to the private home of the chief judge of the District Court, who was also a graduate of M University in Tokyo. In a casual yet somewhat more direct manner this time, he intended to ask for a transfer to the District Court, which he'd been requesting for a long time.

At the meeting about the security situation in each area, he tried to get this message across by directly declaring to the chief judge, who appeared to be nodding off, that the "bands" of communists had been completely wiped out under his jurisdiction. There was no need to worry about them causing any more mischief, he added.

In point of fact, there were no longer any political prisoners or thought criminals locked up in the police stations in his jurisdiction. During the year or so since he'd assumed his post, he'd gotten rid of all of them.

Until, that is, he came back and found this incident waiting for him. No wonder he was so upset. To make matters worse, he heard it was that damn Pak Tal again!

Enraptured as always by the sound of his own footsteps, Kim Nam-ch'ŏl stomped up the stairs even more loudly than usual this morning. On the second floor, he flung open the office door—which was marked with a nameplate that read "Public Prosecutor for Law and Order"—and stormed in, throwing his briefcase on the desk with a thud.

"Call the chief at the station. Tell him I'm on my way," he barked at an office girl who was tidying up the room. Then, peeking into the office next door, he saw that the chief prosecutor and Prosecutor Ri weren't there yet.

"Hey, where's the clerk?" he asked the office girl, who had gone over to the telephone.

"Yes, he should be here any minute now."

"Hmm."

Kim Nam-ch'ŏl didn't mind that the clerk wasn't in yet, but he couldn't put up with the fact that Prosecutor Ri hadn't shown up to work yet. The prosecutor had probably gone out with the chief again last night and had a few too many drinks with some local shopkeepers. You could hardly call them public prosecutors when all they did was fight economic crime and petty theft. *A cop could easily take care of those things*, he thought, which calmed him down a little.

Given the choice, he preferred going over to the police station himself to do interrogations. Most of all, he liked the air of formality when he set foot in the police station.

"All rise! Salute the public prosecutor!"

When the police officers in the station saw it was him, they sprang to their feet at once. As he walked by them, he would raise his hand magnanimously, as if to tell them not to stand on ceremony, but sometimes he dispensed with the niceties altogether and hurried into the police chief's office or went right up to the second floor, where the interrogation room was. Today, it was the latter.

Kim Nam-ch'ŏl went straight into the interrogation room, which had been a martial arts room during the Japanese colonial period. Back in the old days it used to have a Shintō altar dedicated to the Inner Shrine at Ise and other deities, as well as kendō equipment lined up against the wall. When they weren't being used for kendō, the wooden swords sometimes doubled as torture devices, but those things were all gone now. The wooden swords were still there, of course, but now they were reserved solely for torturing people. Not only were the ropes attached to the rafters still hanging there, just like in the old days, but there was also an assortment of implements used for beating people lined up against the wall. Among them was a dried bull pizzle that had been used way back in the Joseon Dynasty.

Apparently, everything had to be Korean style. Or rather, South Korean style. Back in the Joseon Dynasty, there was a fairly loose system of punishment called a "whipping boy" (someone who would get lashed in place of someone else), but that sort of thing no longer existed. Even if it did, it wasn't commonly used for people deemed political prisoners and thought criminals, either now or back then. After all, crimes of conscience were always the most serious crimes you could commit in this country.

Next, Chief of Law and Order Sama Umun burst into the interrogation room. He quickly saluted Public Prosecutor Kim. Unusually for a Korean, this fellow had a two-character surname (Sama, 司馬), so even during the so-called name-changing campaign of the Japanese colonial period, he didn't have to change his surname to a Japanese one. He was a policeman at that time, and he liked the Japanese film *The Detective Records of Umon*, starring Arashi Kanjūrō, so he simply changed his given name to Umun, using the same characters in the protagonist's name Umon (右門).

Moreover, just like the surname Sama, the name Umun was pronounced almost the same in both Korean and Japanese, so even now he thought it was the best name in the entire world. Actually, after August 15, 1945, he secretly wondered how to say his name in English. When he asked someone, he was surprised to be told, "It's just Umun Sama." "Umun Sama. That sounds like Umun-*sama*, 'The Honorable Mr. Umon,' in Japanese," he said with a laugh, even prouder of himself.

Despite having such an auspicious name, he was a little dissatisfied that he was still just a chief and a guard (at the rank of lieutenant) in the Law and Order Section. Deep down inside, he resented being bossed around by a whippersnapper like Public Prosecutor Kim Nam-ch'ŏl, who would tell him to do this and do that. Just now, Sama thought Kim might drop by his office and tell him to do something else, but Kim just walked by his office and went straight into the interrogation room.

Sama told himself it was pointless to get upset about it. After all, Kim was an upstart "liberation-era public prosecutor," so he only cared about getting ahead in the world and knew nothing about social graces.

"What brings you here so early in the morning?" Sama asked, acting surprised. "Man, you public prosecutors never stop working, do you? You make the rest of us look like slackers. Hahaha . . ."

"Are you done with the jokes? If so, go get that lunatic,"
Kim Nam-ch'ŏl said.

"Lunatic? Oh, you mean Pak Tal?" Sama said, slightly
miffed but still feigning ignorance. "If that's who you're
talking about, we grilled him a little yesterday, but he
screamed again as usual. Honestly, we don't know what to
do with him."

The message behind Sama's words was loud and clear:
*You know, it's still our job to interrogate that guy, not
yours. I'll send the report over to the Public Prosecutor's
Office, so you can just read that. Why do you keep coming
over here in the first place . . . ?*

Kim Nam-ch'ŏl, though, had his mind on something
else. *If it was a petty thief or something, that would be one
thing, but this is a despicable political prisoner and thought
criminal. There's no way in hell I'm leaving this up to a
bunch of low-ranking civil servants like you*, he thought.

"I don't care, just bring him out here on the double."

"Hey! Go get Pak Tal!" Sama shouted as he turned
on his heel and walked out, as if to say, *I can boss people
around, too, ya know.* A patrolman rushed out of the
Office of the Chief of Law and Order next door and ran

up to him.

"Bring me Pak Tal."

"Yessir."

The patrolman went downstairs to the jail. Until two days ago it had been jam-packed with workers, some of them even spilling into the hallway, but now there were only seventeen or eighteen leaders of the union in there, such as Chŏn Sang-t'aek. The police probably would have wanted to leave them all locked up like that forever, but the American base authorities were the first ones to throw in the towel.

Operations on the base were in a complete state of paralysis. The commanding officer Lieutenant Colonel Kirk had no choice but to order the release of all the workers except for those in charge of the union, which is why the only prisoners left were the seventeen or eighteen people regarded as union leaders. Before long, the patrolman came back from the jail accompanied by Pak Tal, whose eyelids were swollen black and blue, perhaps from the previous day's "grilling."

When Pak Tal saw Kim Nam-ch'ŏl standing there, he nodded his head in a slight bow and laughed, "It's been a while, Sir. Thanks for your hard work again today. Eh-heh-heh . . ."

He came closer to Kim Nam-ch'ŏl, still nodding his head obsequiously. His face looked weird and slightly creepy due to the purplish bruises around his eyes. He spotted a tiny piece of thread stuck to the lapel of the public prosecutor's jacket and tried to remove it for him.

Kim Nam-ch'ŏl had been through this routine before, so he immediately pulled back and picked it off himself. Without saying a word, he grinned, letting one gold filling gleam from between his clenched teeth, and decked Pak Tal.

"Uwaaaah!"

Pak Tal toppled over theatrically, seemingly caught off guard. With impeccable timing, he hit the ground and stopped moving altogether, as though he were dead. Through his half-closed eyelids, however, he was watching the public prosecutor's every move.

Their "struggle" had been going on for what seemed like days now. Even so, this was only the third time that Kim Nam-ch'ŏl had interrogated Pak Tal directly. During that period, though, he had also interrogated Chŏn Sang-t'aek and Ch'oe Tong-kil for days on end. Plus, this wasn't the first time he'd interrogated Pak Tal—there was the previous time and the time before that—but each session seemed to blend into the next, separated only by time, so for the two of them it felt like they'd been going at it for days.

To make matters worse, it was always the same routine, over and over again. Now, after so many days of this, even Kim Nam-ch'ŏl seemed to be getting tired: he was panting like a dog as he wiped the sweat from his brow. He'd completely forgotten about his gentlemanly appearance. No matter how hot it was, he normally never took off his suit jacket or undid his necktie, but now he'd taken both of them off and was sitting astride a round wooden stool, trying to catch his breath as his shoulders heaved. In one hand, he gripped the bull pizzle whip, which had been soaked in water to give it more elasticity. At his feet lay Pak Tal, whose hands were handcuffed and whose long, lanky body was sprawled across the floor.

Pak Tal was completely naked save for a pair of filthy underpants that were starting to fall apart. In that state, his six-foot frame looked quite muscular, as one might expect from someone with such a build, but his body was covered with bloody red welts from the whip—all the

178

THE TRIAL OF PAK TAL AND OTHER STORIES

way down to his lower abdomen—as though someone had dragged a hot iron across his skin, making him look somewhat gruesome. Like a dead frog, he lay belly up looking at the ceiling, bubbles of blood swelling from his blisters with every breath.

Having realized that the two men were taking a break, the patrolman from the Office of the Chief of Law and Order brought Kim Nam-ch'ŏl yet another glass of sweetened ice water. The patrolman was young and inexperienced, so he timidly offered the ice water to the public prosecutor while trying not to look at the grotesque sight of Pak Tal splayed out on the floor. Just then, Pak Tal, who had been watching the patrolman, abruptly sat up.

"Mr. Policeman, how 'bout bringin' me a glass o' water, too? I don't need no sugar in it. Eh-heh . . ." Pak Tal tried to laugh, but the muscles in his swollen face suddenly froze up.

The patrolman glanced at the public prosecutor's face. Kim Nam-ch'ŏl was drinking his ice water in silence. So the patrolman went back to his office and got a glass of water for Pak Tal as well.

Pak Tal held out his cuffed hands and took the glass

The Trial of Pak Tal

of water. While he was at it, he twisted his swollen face into a bizarre grin and thrust his hands out even farther toward the patrolman. He was pleading with him to loosen the handcuffs a little, as his writhing around on the floor earlier had tightened them. The patrolman glanced at the public prosecutor's face again and then quickly loosened them. This may have been Pak Tal's real aim, not the water.

"What the hell are you talking about?" Kim Nam-ch'ŏl started in again, after each of them had finished their waters. "Why do you keep saying the same damn thing over and over? Huh? Tell me!"

"Eh-heh-heh . . . Are we starting already, Sir? Isn't it a bit early? Let's rest a little more—" Pak Tal started to say, but Kim Nam-ch'ŏl cut him off.

"Idiot! You never learn, do you?"

Kim Nam-ch'ŏl took the bull pizzle whip in his hand and stood up.

"Okay, okay, I'll tell you, I'll tell you," Pak Tal said, quickly raising his handcuffed hands to hold Kim off. "I'll tell you. I'll tell you, but I thought you might be getting tired, Sir."

"Get to the point! What is it? Why? I don't have all day,

you know."

"Well, Sir, it's like I've been telling you all along. It's basically the same thing. You won't get mad at me, will you, Sir? You always get so angry. Eh-heh-heh . . ."

"You stupid idiot! What the hell are you trying to say? Spit it out already!"

Kim Nam-ch'ŏl's face was flushed with anger, and his erect body was trembling with rage. He was a relatively short-tempered person, but anyone would lose their cool in this kind of situation.

"You really won't get mad at me?"

"I said tell me, goddammit!" Kim yelled, even more irritated. Wasn't he worried about having an epileptic seizure?

"That's, uh, eh-heh-heh . . . That's because you gentlemen get so angry all the time. That's why," Pak Tal said calmly, turning away. Out of the corner of his eye, he was watching the expression on Kim Nam-ch'ŏl's face.

"What? Because I get angry?" Kim recoiled for a moment, feeling as if he were in a fairy tale or something. "Because I get angry . . . ? In that case, shouldn't you just stop doing things like that?"

"No, it's not that easy. You gentlemen just need to stop

getting angry at us."

"What did you just say? The only reason we get angry at you is because you keep doing those things without ever learning your lesson. As long as you just shut up and do your job like you're supposed to, no one will get angry at you. Why is that so hard for you to understand?"

"No, that's not the way it works. You have it backwards. If you gentlemen would stop getting angry, everything would be fine."

"What?! Why you little . . . !" Kim Nam-ch'ŏl said, his body trembling again and his eyes opening wide. "What on earth do you think the law is?"

Kim finally seemed to understand what Pak Tal was saying. Pak Tal's words were a frightening form of insurrection against the law itself. They were also, therefore, an open act of defiance toward Kim himself. He was the Public Prosecutor for Law and Order, after all.

Kim Nam-ch'ŏl raised the thick bull pizzle whip in his hand. He brought it down hard. It sounded like someone slapping freshly pounded *mochi*.

"Take that, you little son of a bitch!"

Once he began whipping, a strange kind of hatred seemed to take control of him, and the rest was a blur of flogging. Blood spurted from Pak Tal's shoulders. It also dripped from the end of the whip, scattering across the floor.

"W-w-wait a minute, wait a minute! Uwaaaah!"

Raising his handcuffed hands to deflect the whip, Pak Tal rolled around, writhing on the floor. Sometimes he screamed, "Uwaaaah!" in a loud, booming voice.

He also said things like "Help me!" and "You murderer!"

Of course, his cries echoed throughout the police station. At times, his screams could even be heard outside the station as well, causing passersby to stop and prick up their ears.

"It's Pak Tal. It's Pak Tal," they would whisper to each other.

Even as he screamed at the top of his lungs, he still shifted his body this way and that on the floor, trying to escape Kim Nam-ch'ŏl's whip.

Try as he might to escape it, however, he knew he must never steer clear of it completely.

By doing so, Pak Tal deftly avoided being hit in his vitals, although in this case it might be more appropriate to say he manipulated Kim into not hitting his vitals.

The Trial of Pak Tal

Otherwise, he would have found himself in a far worse world of pain. With his wealth of experience from before, he knew every trick in the book when it came to torture.

Therefore, even amid all that writhing, he let himself be hit on purpose once every three times or so. In other words, even as he was trying to escape, he had to give his opponent a suitable amount of satisfaction from the whipping.

"Shut your trap, you little loudmouth! I've waited long enough for you. If you have something to say, then say it!"

Once Kim's entire body felt the satisfaction of whipping someone two times in a row, he stood still, gasping for breath. Meanwhile, Pak Tal was picking up steam, still writhing on the floor as he screamed, "Uwaaaah! Uwaaaah!"

"Sir, w-w-wait a minute. I don't think I can take much more."

When Pak Tal noticed that Kim Nam-ch'ŏl had stopped brandishing the whip, he changed his voice completely and began panting as he spoke. Even so, his eyes moved quickly, constantly checking the expression on Kim's face. *Wow*, he thought, *this guy's really going at it today* . . . .

"What do you mean wait, you little bastard? I should kill someone like you! Next time, you're getting the death penalty!"

"W-wait! If that's the case, then this is even more important. I still . . . I still haven't told you the whole story. You have to hear the rest of it!"

"Quit yammering. What haven't you told me? Tell me!"

Kim Nam-ch'ŏl looked as if he were ready to call it a day. As he did before, he pulled the stool over and sat down again. Also as before, he sat there trying to catch his breath while his shoulders heaved.

At his feet lay Pak Tal, sprawled out across the floor. This, too, was the same situation we observed a little while ago. This time, however, Pak Tal was covered in blood. The welts from the recent whipping on his shoulders and elsewhere had burst open and spewed blood, which had mixed with his sweat and spread all over his body while he was rolling around on the floor. Furthermore, he was letting out strange moans that sounded like a dog whimpering: "Uhhn, uhhn."

Watching him do this irked Kim Nam-ch'ŏl beyond belief, and he yelled, "What's wrong with you? Just spit it out!"

You think I'm gonna fall for that, you son of a bitch?
Kim said to himself. At the same time, he suddenly
thought, *Why the hell does this lunatic have to be such a*
pain in the ass? He's like a little tick that just won't let go.

"Sir, how am I supposed to spit it out when I can't even
sit up? Do you mind if I talk lying down?"

According to Korean custom, the only people who can
talk while lying down are adults speaking to children—
in other words, superiors to inferiors. And the people
who are fussiest about this sort of thing are precisely
government officials and public prosecutors like Kim
Nam-ch'ŏl.

Again, just as before, the patrolman from the Office
of the Chief of Law and Order brought in a glass of
sweetened ice water for the public prosecutor. When he
saw Pak Tal lying there covered in blood and moaning,
"Uhhn, uhhn," he stopped dead in his tracks.

"Get outta here! We're fine!" Kim Nam-ch'ŏl barked at
the patrolman, waving him away. The patrolman quickly
backed out the door, spilling the water in the cup as he left.

During interrogations by the public prosecutor at the
police station, it was standard practice for someone else to
be present to record the proceedings—such as the police

chief, a section chief, or a patrolman—but Kim refused to let in anyone from the police force except in special circumstances. He rightfully believed that the whole lot of them were corrupt elements who were only interested in lining their own pockets with bribes.

As a result, Kim Nam-ch'ŏl was completely isolated, not only from his own department but also from the police. In his isolation, he'd grown even more obstinate. Thus, even the frequent delivery of ice water from Sama Umun's office might have felt like a kind of harassment, depending on how he took it.

"You have some nerve . . . . Stop trying to annoy me. I know exactly what you're talking about. Now sit up straight and spit it out!"

Once Kim Nam-ch'ŏl saw that the patrolman was gone, he nudged Pak Tal in the side with the tip of his boot.

"Ouch, ouch! I'm not trying to annoy you, Sir. Try putting yourself in my shoes, just for a moment. If it were you, Sir, who'd been beaten by me with a bull's balls till you were covered in blood, would you be able to sit up straight and talk to me?"

Pak Tal's eyes looked up at Kim from the middle of

his dreadful face, which was swollen all over and horribly misshapen. Blood was trickling from the corner of his left eye.

"Say something, you bastard! Okay, if you won't get up, then get the hell away from me!" Kim Nam-ch'ŏl said, grabbing the bull pizzle whip again as he quickly rose to his feet. At the same time, he kicked Pak Tal as hard as he could.

Pak Tal, however, was quicker. He twisted his body around and rolled away, narrowly avoiding Kim's foot. Then, without missing a beat, he abruptly sat up at a right angle.

"I'll get up. I'm sitting up, aren't I? Sir, I can't even talk to you because you always get so angry. You really should control that temper of yours."

"What did you say to me . . . ?"

Kim Nam-ch'ŏl stood there for a moment glaring at Pak Tal, but then he sat down on the stool, as if he'd changed his mind. Perhaps it was the heat, but he suddenly felt dizzy and exhausted.

"Listen, the reason I get so angry," he began, his words taking on a different tone. "As I've said to you time and time again, I'm angry because of the law. You've violated the rule of law. And not just once or twice either. Why the hell can't you understand that?"

"Because I just can't, Sir. You can talk about the law or the rule of law all you want, but they don't mean a thing to an ignorant and uneducated man like me. The only thing folks like me understand is whether gentlemen like you are angry or not. That's it, Sir."

As he said this, Pak Tal closed his left eye, which was dripping blood, and stared straight through the public prosecutor with his other eye. Deep in his heart, he was thinking, *What the hell are you talking about, you idiot? The rule of law doesn't mean a damn thing; it's just something you made up to suit yourselves. And everyone knows you're just a watchdog anyway, not the one who really makes the rules around here . . . .*

In this way, the lessons that Pak Tal had learned from his "teachers" in that jail and detention center ran through his mind one after another. Even so, it was a formidable monologue. Had Kim Nam-ch'ŏl been able to hear Pak Tal's inner voice at that moment, he would have jumped out of his seat for sure.

Ignorance truly is bliss, as they say. Meanwhile, Pak Tal continued to think to himself: *Hmph, the guy seems to be getting tired. Well then, I guess it's time to start the real show. No, wait, maybe I should put him through a few more rounds. No, no, I think he's had enough. But damn, that hurt like hell today.*

At this point, it became hard to tell who was interrogating whom. No wonder Kim Nam-ch'ŏl's head was starting to hurt.

"Pak Tal, if that's what you think, let me remind you of something. I'm always angry at you, right? Has there ever been a time when I didn't get angry at you? In other words, the law is always angry at you. But you always do the same thing: bow your head hundreds of times and say, I'll never do it again, I'll mend my ways, please just this once . . . Am I wrong?"

Kim seemed completely worn out, for his voice had taken on an unusually persuasive tone all of a sudden. It was the kind of persuasive tone he rarely used even toward his own wife.

When you think about it, maybe that kind of tone was precisely the point of interrogations like this. In Kim Nam-ch'ŏl's case, though, he appeared to be at his wit's end with this man who made no sense to him. Every time he interrogated Pak Tal, not just this time, he had no idea why he got so angry and worked up by the end.

It was clear that Pak Tal had committed a crime. He wasn't denying it, nor was he hiding it. Nor did it seem like he had any particular underlying motive or hidden agenda. In other words, he was shallow-minded. First of all, why would such a guy do something like this . . . ? And who told him to do this . . . ? Kim thought, going through all the possible explanations—from A to Z—to figure out why Pak Tal did what he did.

That, however, is where Kim Nam-ch'ŏl made a crucial mistake. As the writer, I must confess to being rather delighted by his mistake or misunderstanding. Kim believed that Pak Tal was shallow-minded because there was no deeper explanation for what he did, but actually, what Kim failed to realize was that Pak Tal was much smarter than he seemed precisely because he did those things for no apparent reason and because no one was telling him what to do. This just goes to show Kim's own lack of autonomy as a human being, but what was even more unforgivable was his utter contempt for our hero Pak Tal.

"Nonetheless," Kim Nam-ch'ŏl continued, "what the hell were you thinking? After saying those things, you go

.

right back to your old ways and start causing trouble with all this labor union stuff. On top of that, you go around boasting that you're in charge of the union, that you're the chairman. And those flyers—what were those flyers all about? Did you somehow think I wouldn't get angry about that?"

"That's right, Sir," Pak Tal answered straight away. "I was hoping you wouldn't get angry anymore, Sir. Even though you said all those things to me before, it's been more than six months since then, and I thought that maybe the law—is that what you call it?—had changed during that time. And maybe you, too, Sir. Even if it hadn't changed, we would've—I mean, we had no choice but to test it out and see for ourselves using our own bodies. After all, even when the law does change, you gentlemen never notify us of the details."

"Notify you? Who do you think you are, the president?!"

Kim Nam-ch'ŏl picked up the bull pizzle whip again and stood up, his forehead dripping with greasy sweat. His whole body was trembling.

"W-w-wait a minute, Sir. Then I, then I . . ."

"Then you what?"

"Then I realized something. That you were still angry, Sir. Why, of course you were! Why wouldn't you still be angry? And then I thought to myself, eh-heh-heh . . . Sir, I promise I will never, ever do it again."

I'm gonna pay for that, Pak Tal thought, and let out a loud belly laugh while secretly bracing himself. And sure enough, he did!

"What did you say to me?!" Kim Nam-ch'ŏl said, summoning all of his strength and brandishing the whip again.

"Who the hell do you think I am? I'm the public prosecutor. How dare you speak to a government official like that, you little son of a bitch!"

In short, it was the same old thing all over again. This time, however, the situation was a bit—no, quite a bit—different. Pak Tal's voice suddenly changed from laughter to cries.

"Sir, pleeease! I won't do it anymore. I told you I won't do it anymore. I'll never do it again, I promise! Uwaaaah! Uwaaaah! Sir, pleeease! Somebody, help me! I'll won't do it again!"

As usual, Pak Tal was rolling around all over the floor . . . At that point, though, a major change took place. Kim

Nam-ch'ŏl, with his whip raised above his head, suddenly began convulsing and then collapsed on the floor.

Kim was lying on his back, mumbling something incoherent and foaming at the mouth. Apparently, he'd suffered a seizure from his chronic epilepsy. Amid the heat and multiple days of working himself too hard, he must have gotten overexcited. One of his legs was twitching spasmodically.

Even Pak Tal was surprised by this turn of events. Holding up his cuffed hands, he got on his knees and shuffled across the floor toward Kim Nam-ch'ŏl. He gazed at Kim's face for a while with a look of disbelief. Eventually, he went over to the door at the entrance, lay down again, and called out to the hallway. "Sir . . . Chief, the public prosecutor's gone to sleep."

"What? The public prosecutor fell asleep?!"

Led by Chief of Law and Order Sama Umun, a bunch of patrolmen stormed into the room. The police station was thrown into chaos.

As he listened to the commotion behind him, Pak Tal crawled down the stairs from the second floor accompanied by the patrolman who had brought him a glass of water earlier. Covered in blood and clad only in

THE TRIAL OF PAK TAL AND OTHER STORIES

his underpants, he crawled along the long hallway toward the jail, using the elbow of one arm, which had been uncuffed. The cold, smooth surface of the concrete floor felt nice against his skin.

Serves you right, you bastard, he thought to himself, barely suppressing a laugh that welled up in his belly. Numerous times, he chuckled, "Eh-heh-heh" at the kind-looking young patrolman who followed along behind him. Perhaps he thought about standing up right then and there and marching down the hall.

But Pak Tal quietly restrained himself and crawled on, letting out those strange moans of "Uhhn, uhhn" as he savored the cold sensation of the floor against his skin. The young patrolman followed along silently behind him, with a touch of sympathy on his face.

At the door to the jail, the patrolman stepped out in front of Pak Tal and opened it. Inside, the jail was filled with guards. First up on the left-hand side was the women's cell. Farther down, past the toilets, were the men's cells: a lone line of iron doors.

Tan-sŏn peered out from within the women's cell, clinging to the grating of the iron door with both hands. For the past few hours, each time the jail door opened, she'd ran to the door and looked out through the bars, waiting for Pak Tal to be brought back. Following her example, a number of other women were gathered around the door.

"Hey, it's Mr. Pak Tal," somebody said. Tan-sŏn pressed her face against the iron grating.

When Pak Tal reached her cell, crawling along the floor and letting out the same moans of "Uhhn, uhhn" as usual, he abruptly stopped moaning. Like a snake lifting its head up, he looked toward the women's cell.

Then, like a crippled man who suddenly rises up and starts walking, he stood up and walked straight over to Tan-sŏn's cell. Locking his fingers with hers through the openings in the iron grating, he whispered, "Don't worry, I'm fine." The guards—who'd been watching with bated breath as he crawled down the hallway covered in blood from head to toe—quickly rushed over and pried the two of them apart.

Pak Tal crawled down the hall toward his own cell, once again moaning, "Uhhn, uhhn." Tan-sŏn saw him off in silence, with no emotion on her face except for her fiercely gleaming eyes.

"My, how horrible!"

"Isn't that awful?"

Mixed in with these voices of the other women was one belonging to a young female student named Yu Pang-sun. She'd been arrested for "who knows what reason," as she put it, on her way back home from Keijō (Seoul) for summer vacation. Now she covered her face and burst into tears. The mere sight of Pak Tal covered in blood had sent shivers through her entire body.

Tan-sŏn, though, didn't move at all. She'd kept her mouth shut the entire time, from the day she was arrested and thrown in jail until now. She knew Pak Tal's "secrets" better than anyone. Now that she was his partner—in life and in crime—she knew she must never leave his side.

Tan-sŏn, too, had been dragged out for questioning once by Public Prosecutor Kim Nam-ch'ŏl, and she'd been punched and kicked by Chief Sama Umun as well, but she never opened her mouth the entire time. She was one tough cookie.

The cell Pak Tal was put into was one he knew well: Cell #5 at the very end. Among the other people in there with him were Chŏn Sang-t'aek and Yun T'ae-yŏng, who were connected to the recent labor union incident. Now there were only eighteen people left, including Tan-sŏn, who were tied to the incident and thought to be responsible for the union, but there were only five cells, so it was impossible to split them up individually.

When Pak Tal crawled into the cell, Ri Sŭng, a pickpocket who had been caught on his way from Pusan to Keijō (Seoul), said, "Well, look who we have here . . . . You got pretty messed up today, too, huh?" Pak Tal grinned at him, giving him a little wink with one eye.

Inside the cell, Chŏn Sang-t'aek and Yun T'ae-yŏng were already asleep, lying side by side. Both of them had been interrogated by Kim Nam-ch'ŏl until the day before, and the results were not pretty. Of the two, Chŏn Sang-t'aek was in particularly bad shape. Apparently, they thought there was something fishy about him, so they'd hung him upside down and tortured him to get more information about his background.

Pak Tal threaded his way through the inmates crowding the cell and joined his sleeping buddies.

"You're hurt pretty bad . . ." Chŏn Sang-t'aek said as he softly touched Pak Tal with his right hand, unable to open his eyes and see for himself because even his eyes had been hurt during the interrogation.

"What are you talking about? This is nothing. What's

worse is, it was so funny that I . . . Ah, ouch, hold on. Damn, that hurts. Okay, I'm fine. It was so funny I nearly split my sides. The guy just fell over like a log."

For someone who had been making strange moans of "Uhhn, uhhn" until just a few moments ago, Pak Tal was a completely different person. His body still ached, though, as one might expect.

"What guy?"

"You know, the public prosecutor guy. I thought about putting him through a few more paces with me, but he passed out before I could."

"Hey, he's here," Ri Sŭng said, turning his head away from the door, where he was sitting. The guard had come by to check on them.

"Pak Tal . . ." Chŏn Sang-t'aek said, once the guard's footsteps had faded into the distance. "I know I've said this many times before, but when it comes to the recent strike, would you mind not being so eager to cover for me? I'll take full responsibility for it this time. After all, I was prepared to do that from the beginning. So let me handle this . . . ."

"Sure. You weren't offended or anything by me saying I was the chairman, were you?"

"Don't be ridiculous! Why would I be offended by something like that? That's not what I mean. I finally realized something after being put in jail and tortured. This should have happened to me much earlier. I don't know if you can understand this or not, but I'm finally relieved that they caught me."

Chŏn Sang-t'aek spoke in a serious tone, emphasizing each and every word. Tears flowed from the corners of both of his eyes, which were swollen shut.

"What are you talking about? You sound like one of those so-called intellectuals. If that's what you think, it's no use arguing with you, but that's not the way I see it. If I get arrested, the only thing I care about is getting out of here as quick as I can. I don't know if I'd call it a relief, but if I were stuck in a place like this, I wouldn't be able to do much of anything."

Pak Tal looked at the high ceiling, as though he were talking to himself. But that's what he thought.

Chŏn Sang-t'aek, meanwhile, had his own thoughts on the matter. He seemed to have some kind of deeper reasons for thinking the way he did. People secretly thought he might be a member of the underground Workers' Party, so maybe he did have some personal affairs of that nature that he couldn't share with the others.

Such as how, at a certain decisive moment, he'd betrayed his comrades against his will, or something like that . . . . No matter how strong-willed these men were, they were still human beings after all, so such things could happen, especially in the cold, hard world of reality. Perhaps, if I tried digging a little deeper, that might become another story, but until then this writer has his hands full with this one. That story will have to wait for another day.

In short, the eighteen people who remained here in custody each had their own ideas about what they did, and their own reasons for what they did. Not all of them could be like Pak Tal. On the whole, though, they were all much more energetic than any of us could imagine.

They were divided into twos and threes among the five cells, but, as anyone who has ever set foot in one of these jails knows, they still found a way to pass along news about each other. From what they heard, the liveliest among them, other than Pak Tal, was Secretary-General Ch'oe Tong-kil, which came as no surprise.

Here is what they heard from him: "The next chance

I get, I'm definitely going to escape from here, so don't worry about me at all" and "If I can't escape from here, I'll break out of prison." There was something quite frightening about the man, but compared to him, Ri Chŏng-chu seemed completely spineless, unlike the characters in his given name (正柱), which meant "upright pillar."

If anything, it appeared that Ri Chŏng-chu was being encouraged and consoled by Old Man Cho Sŏk-u and the others, not the other way around. "Dog guard" Chŏn Man-sŏk was pissed off about this, but he'd always been a bit of a loose cannon.

Before long, summer ended, and autumn deepened across southern Korea. During that time, nothing really happened in this town, at least on the surface. Then, one winter day, a public hearing for Pak Tal and the others was held at the court. Even though it was called a "public hearing," it was very different from the kind of open court that all of us have seen or imagined.

In the trials we're used to seeing, witnesses take the stand and testify, prosecutors and lawyers quibble with each other about the testimony, and prosecutors present their closing arguments at the end. In this court, however, at least as far as political prisoners and thought criminals were concerned, nobody ever had a chance to see that kind of trial. In a public hearing, in other words, everything had been wrapped up before it even began. At least, it was supposed to be wrapped up.

Therefore, the only part of the proceedings that relatives and townspeople connected to the defendant were allowed to attend was this final public hearing, where the decision was announced. Even that, however, was normally conducted in secret, with as little public notification as possible. Unless you had a really reliable lawyer, it was all over in the blink of eye, before anyone knew it.

Earlier, I touched upon the unique character of Yu Yong-dŏk, the chief judge of this court, or more precisely, the K Branch of the M District Court. Even for a chief judge like him, though, there was little he could do about this. It was a systemic issue. The more good-natured he was, the harder it was to change the system.

In the case of the trial of Pak Tal and the others, however, the situation was a little different. Or completely different, you might say. Almost every single person in the town (including the proprietress of that bar) quietly contributed money to hire two lawyers who really had their act together. Perhaps for that reason, word traveled fast about the public hearing until the entire town knew about it.

They also knew the public prosecutor's closing arguments and recommended sentence, which (as a matter of course) had been filed in advance. So, a group of townspeople got together to come up with a plan, led by the recently released Yun T'ae-yǒng and Cho Sǒk-u. Since there would be a crackdown if too many people showed up at once, and since they would be put at an even greater disadvantage if the hearing were postponed for that reason, they decided—after many discussions—to choose fifty observers, the maximum number allowed. Interestingly, only those with extremely sharp and steady eyes were qualified to be selected.

Ultimately, six people were prosecuted in this trial: Chǒn Sang-t'aek, the highest-ranking member of the union; Ri Chǒng-chu; Ch'oe Tong-kil (who still hadn't been able to make his big escape); Chǒn Man-sǒk; Tan-sǒn, who was charged with "affixing deplorable flyers under the instigation of her lawless husband with no qualms whatsoever"; and Pak Tal. The others had finally been released right before the trial. Among all the defendants, though, the one Kim Nam-ch'ŏl felt the most hatred for was none other than our hero Pak Tal. The next was Tan-sŏn, who had remained tight-lipped to the bitter end in his interrogation.

The penalty he asked for was harshest for these two. All six were being charged under the National Security Act, but Kim Nam-ch'ŏl said this about Pak Tal at the end of his closing argument: "Thus, while not entirely beyond the realm of possibility, the defendant's antinational and antisocial disposition and character cannot possibly be rectified easily. Accordingly, it is hereby determined that a sentence of ten years is reasonable." The only thing I can understand from this legal gobbledygook is that he asked for a ten-year sentence.

And so today was the day when the decision would finally be handed down. The fifty chosen observers crowded into the courthouse in advance, waiting for the court to open. There were fifty of them exactly, not one missing . . . no, wait, that's odd. Not one of them was speaking.

Even at something as somber as a funeral, when fifty

people got together like this, there would usually be a lot of noise and chatter, but these people didn't say a single word to each other. It was like—how shall I put it?—a bunch of mummies had come and were standing completely still in the hallway of the courthouse. They didn't move a muscle. The court attendant—an old man they'd known for years—came out from inside and exclaimed, "My goodness, what a crowd. What's goin' on this mornin'?" as he opened the courtroom doors for them, but they didn't say a word to him either. They filed in slowly, their feet not making a sound. They were like ghosts. Once the court attendant determined that the public gallery was full, he retreated into the courtroom chambers with a puzzled look on his face.

The public gallery in the courtroom was of course filled to capacity with the observers, who sat in precise rows, occupying every seat. Still, they didn't say a word. Nor did they move a muscle. In fact, they were so quiet that no one in the courthouse even realized they were there, apart from the court attendant.

The defendants entered the courtroom from the doorway on the right-hand side, led by Pak Tal. Tan-sǒn, who had been separated from him, came in last, walking

THE TRIAL OF PAK TAL AND OTHER STORIES

behind Ri Chŏng-chu. They all looked healthy and full of life compared to when they were being tortured back in that police station jail.

As usual, Pak Tal was a little pudgy, having put on a few pounds since we last saw him. In handcuffs and roped together, they were led in by six patrolmen. They came in without realizing there were any observers in the courtroom, so when they saw them in the public gallery, they almost tripped over themselves for a second. Pak Tal couldn't help but grin.

And what did the observers do? All fifty of them responded by grinning in unison. That was it, though. Then they wiped the smiles from their face and just sat there, staring at the judge's bench with daggers in their eyes. (Only people with sharp and steady eyes had been chosen, so you might say it made for a spectacular sight.)

The cops accompanying the defendants were getting antsy, already feeling outnumbered by those silent gazes. The defendants, however, knew what those watchful eyes meant. They themselves were a little uneasy at first, turning around and looking at all the people in the public gallery from time to time, but when they realized why those people were there, they hung their heads in

The Trial of Pak Tal

silence—as if they'd discussed this beforehand—and fell still. They were deeply moved.

It was even more emotional for Pak Tal. He hung his head and cried, his tears dripping loudly onto the floor below. That was understandable. And as it should be. Until just now, he'd always been by himself, alone in the world. He was surprised and impressed by how tough his own wife, Tan-sŏn, was, but he'd never experienced such widespread concern and support for his actions before.

Yes, this is what I've been fighting for. And this is what I'll continue to fight for, Pak Tal thought. He felt as though he'd finally reached the end of a very long journey.

He felt the urge to fire off another "Eh-heh-heh" in a full-bellied voice as loud as he could, but he tightly pressed his lips together and held it in. Perhaps he'd gained an awareness of himself as part of a larger group, as it were, for the first time in his life.

The door on the right side opened and the judges strode out, led by Chief Judge Yu Yong-dŏk. Public Prosecutor Kim Nam-ch'ŏl, apparently cured of his epilepsy, came out next from the doorway on the left. Then, all at once, they stopped dead in their tracks. They were stunned by the unexpected eyes of the observers

THE TRIAL OF PAK TAL AND OTHER STORIES

staring at them in silent judgment.

Pak Tal forced himself not to laugh . . . .

Well, dear readers, I should probably tell you how this trial ends, but here I've decided to put down my pen for the time being. That's because, no matter what happens, our hero Pak Tal probably won't get out of serving a few years in prison this time. It's not that I can't bear to watch him go to prison. Rather, I can't wait to see what happens after he finishes his sentence and gets out. He'll surely show up in this society again at some point.

The word "sentence" makes it sound like a long time, but it probably won't be more than, say, two years or so because the person doing the sentencing was the "cowardly" Yu Yong-dŏk, who was now holding the written judgment in his shaking hands as the silent, immovable eyes of the observers fell upon him. Whenever it came time to read a decision, he had a habit of often—if not always—misreading the final numbers.

For example, when he was supposed to say five years, he'd accidentally say one year, or instead of three years he'd say half a year, which always infuriated Public Prosecutor Kim Nam-ch'ŏl to no end. I'm sure he'll do it again this time. The town of K in southern Korea is an interesting place indeed. No doubt it will become even more interesting the next time Pak Tal gets out of prison. Well, dear readers, let's just wait and see.

All the Way to Tsushima

(Tsushima made, 1975)

The night before we left, Ri Sin-ki and I stayed at Chŏng
Chŏng-mun's place in Kyoto.* The next morning, the
three of us headed to Osaka Airport. We'd already
purchased our plane tickets in advance, so it was just a
hop, skip, and a jump from Osaka to Fukuoka, and then
from Fukuoka to Iki.

Altogether it took about an hour and a half to get
there, although the leg from Fukuoka to Iki, in particular,
was disappointingly short. No sooner had the airplane
taken off than we were already landing at Iki Airport.

---

* Ri Sin-ki is based on the Zainichi Korean historian and writer Yi Chin-hŭi
(李進熙, 1929–2012). Chŏng Chŏng-mun is based on the Zainichi Korean
businessman and art collector Chŏng Cho-mun (鄭詔文, 1918–1989).
Kim made two trips to Tsushima with Yi and Chŏng Cho-mun, first in
late August 1973 and again in late October 1974. This story is a semi-
fictionalized account of both trips. [Translator]

When seen on a map, Iki is a small island in the middle of the Genkai Sea, between Japan and South Korea, but when we stepped off the plane and took a look around, it didn't feel like a tiny remote island at all. Under a cloudless autumn sky, the low, gentle, blue-green mountains spread out as far as the eye could see.

The island looked the same as when we'd passed through it for the first time, about a year earlier. Not much had changed.

We took a taxi to the town of Gōnoura, speeding along a white road that wove its way through those blue-green mountains. There were still no flights all the way to Tsushima, so we had to take a boat from there.

Our plane had arrived at Iki at 4 pm, and the boat to Tsushima was due to leave at 5:30 pm. The boat made a stop here on its way from Fukuoka to Tsushima, crossing paths with the boat that stopped here on its way from Tsushima to Fukuoka. Thus, we still had more than an hour to kill. It was the same way when we'd come here a year earlier. At that time, however, there were five or six other people in our group besides the three of us, so the time went by in a hurry as we chatted noisily among ourselves.

This time, though, it was just the three of us. As the air became thick with our own thoughts and feelings, it felt as if we had too much time on our hands. That said, we didn't really have enough time to go anywhere else.

At first, we each did our own thing, sitting on the benches in the waiting room or checking out the nearby souvenir shops, but in the end, we regrouped and wandered around the harbor together. We tended to keep quiet, no one saying much. We were just trying to pass the time.

If one of us had said something thoughtless—or something honest—the whole basis for this trip to Tsushima might have collapsed at once. For instance, if someone had blurted out, "This is ridiculous. I'm getting on the next boat back to Fukuoka and going home," that might have been the end of it.

The first mistake we made was asking too many questions at the airport in Fukuoka. We'd changed planes there, so we had about thirty minutes between flights. So, after buying some cigarettes in the transit lounge, we took the chance to walk around the airport a little. We hadn't noticed it the previous time, but we happened to spot a young female attendant in a red uniform sitting in front of an electronic signboard announcing the departure times for flights to various countries and regions. The signboard displayed a Korean Air Lines flight to Pusan. Surprised to see Pusan, I approached the young lady in the red uniform and asked, "How long does it take to get to Pusan?"

"Forty minutes," she responded at once.

"Really? And what would a ticket cost . . . ?"

"That would be 9,500 yen," she quickly replied again.

"Did you hear that? 9,500 yen and forty minutes," I said to Chŏng Chŏng-mun and Ri Sin-ki, who were standing beside me. Then I fell silent, not knowing what else to say.

It wasn't as if we hadn't known you could fly to South Korea. We'd known for a long time that "if you leave in the morning, you can have lunch in Korea," as everyone used to say, not just from Fukuoka, but also from places like Tokyo or Osaka.

Even so, when I started to think about it, what we were doing was really ridiculous, even maddening. First of all, the youngest among us was the historian Ri Sin-ki, but even he was in his mid-forties, and Chŏng Chŏng-mun and I were both in our mid-fifties, nearing the start of old age. I imagine this is true for everyone, but when men reach this stage in life, they have various social obligations and become busy with their respective careers.

That was true for me and Ri Sin-ki, who worked as writers, but the businessman Chŏng Chŏng-mun was particularly busy, even more so because he was also the publisher of the journal *Korean Culture of Japan* (Nihon no Chōsen bunka).*

Still, though, why had we come to this faraway island of Iki with no particular purpose other than to wait for a boat to Tsushima? And why were we trying to go even further than that, all the way to the tip of Tsushima . . . ? Even if there was something urgent about this trip for us, when you really thought about it, it was utterly ludicrous—even comical, depending on how you looked at it.

The origin of all this foolishness was our trip to Tsushima a year earlier. Actually, even before that, each of us had dreamed of visiting Tsushima at least once in our lives, thinking, *If we went all the way to Tsushima, then*

---

* Chŏng Cho-mun helped publish the journal *Nihon no naka no Chōsen bunka* (Korean Culture in Japan, 1969–1981). Kim was on the editorial board of this journal. [Translator]

All the Way to Tsushima

maybe we could . . . Apparently, this hope burned like a flame within Ri Sin-ki and Chŏng Chŏng-mun, and I added fuel to the fire.

The reason for this was: I'd heard somewhere a while back—before Chŏng Chŏng-mun began publishing *Korean Culture of Japan* in Kyoto five or six years ago—that if you went all the way to Tsushima, you could see Korea. I used to think maybe that was true, but not really believing it, until two or three years ago, when I went to see a Yayoi period exhibition sponsored by a certain newspaper company at a department store in Tokyo. I found myself riveted by the exhibit, not because the objects exhibited were rare, such as Yayoi vessels or human bones from that period, but because my eyes were drawn to a panel photograph hanging on the wall beside the exhibit. It was an aerial photograph of the ocean with a panoramic view of an island rising up in the center. According to the caption, it was "A View of Korea (Pusan) from Tsushima."

The panel was meant to show the route by which so-called Yayoi culture came into Japan from the Asian continent, but of course I was more interested in the "view." Sure enough, while not as clear as Tsushima in the

THE TRIAL OF PAK TAL AND OTHER STORIES

foreground, the photograph provided a panoramic view of mountains rising on the mainland.

Ah, that must be Pusan, I thought, flushed with emotion. My hometown wasn't far from Pusan. I stood there in front of that panel photograph for what seemed like forever.

When I think about it now, this seems like a silly story as well, but I told it to Chŏng Chŏng-mun and Ri Sinki. After that, whenever the subject of Korea came up in our conversations, someone would often say, "You know, someday I really want to go all the way to Tsushima."

Last year, about a year ago, that dream quickly became a reality because of a study in the journal *Korean Culture of Japan* entitled "Korean-Style Buddhist Imagery and Sculpture" by Kikuchi Jun'ichi, a technical officer with the Ministry of Education at the Nara National Museum. The contents of this study were republished in a newspaper article entitled "Silla Buddhist Statue and Yi Dynasty Written Appointments / Discovered on Tsushima / Awaiting Consideration for Important Cultural Property Designation," which included the following passage:

All the Way to Tsushima

A Buddhist statue, which is thought to have been made on the Korean Peninsula 1,200 years ago, and three "*kokushin*" (letters of appointment), which reveal the history of *wokou* (Japanese pirates), have been discovered on Tsushima in Nagasaki Prefecture. The Agency for Cultural Affairs, which had brought them back to Tokyo for further investigation, recently notified the prefectural Cultural Affairs Division that "Both objects are worth designating as important national cultural properties. They will be submitted to the Council for the Protection of Cultural Properties for consideration." The council will convene on March 18, and the results will be submitted to the Minister of Education on March 22.

The Buddhist statue is a Standing Nyorai (Tathāgata) (38.3 cm tall, made of bronze) that was enshrined at Kaijin Shrine (Chief Priest Torii Tsutae) in Minemura Kisaka.* The statue, a Silla Buddha dating from the early Unified Silla period (668–935), is distinguished by its large head and its ringlet curls (numerous curly hairs), which are smaller than those on Japanese Buddhas. In a report, Nara National Museum Technical

---

* The name Torii Tsutae (鳥居伝) is likely a misspelling of the name Shimai Tsutai (島居伝), who was the chief priest of the Kaijin Shrine at this time. Kaijin Shrine, Facebook direct message to translator, September 11, 2021. [Translator]

Officer Kikuchi Jun'ichi, who was commissioned by the prefecture to examine cultural properties throughout the island of Tsushima, writes, "Silla Buddhas can be found on the Korean Peninsula as well as in Japan, Europe, and North America, but large ones measuring more than thirty centimeters tall are extremely rare. Also, with its stern features and splendidly carved robe, this one probably has no equal on the Korean Peninsula." Not much is known about how it came to Tsushima, but trading ships went back and forth between Korea and Japan at that time, so the most compelling theory is that a crew member offered it to the shrine as a tutelary god of the ocean.

The newspaper article goes on. It's a bit long, but I would like to look at it a little more. Not only does it describe what kind of place Tsushima was—and is—but it also relates to the rest of this story in various ways.

The "*kokushin*" are letters of appointment that the Yi royal family of Korea bestowed upon powerful families of Tsushima to provide them with official ranks and financial support in order to suppress the power of the *wokou* (Japanese pirates). All three letters belonged to Sōda Hideo (52 years old), the principal of

Nii Junior High School, who had kept them in his house at 143 Osaki, Mitsushima-machi, for a long time. One of them is dated "In the 3rd month of the 18th year of the Seonghwa era (1482)," using the Korean era name adopted from the Ming Dynasty. All three letters are stamped with gold seals thought to belong to the Yi royal family. These ancient writings have never been discovered in Japan before, and it is believed there are very few left even on the Korean Peninsula.

Since last November (1972), Tsushima has been linked to Fukuoka via ferry, which has brought a dramatic increase in tourists from all over Kyūshū as well as Tokyo, Osaka, and other places. Approximately 120,000 people visited Tsushima last year, roughly 70% more than the number who visited before the ferry went into service. At the same time, there has been an increase in brokers buying up folkcraft items and Buddhist images passed down in families for generations. For this reason, the Society for Preserving Tsushima's Nature and Culture (President Kotō Mitsuru, 8 chapters, 100 members) has led a movement to protect the island's cultural properties. In August of last year, with the cooperation of the Agency for Cultural Affairs, the prefecture conducted its first formal investigation, which uncovered these artifacts.

THE TRIAL OF PAK TAL AND OTHER STORIES

Since seeing the Kikuchi study, even before this newspaper article, we'd already been formulating an idea in our minds. We wanted to go to Tsushima ourselves, investigate these matters firsthand, and then hold a roundtable discussion based on our findings. The roundtable was for the journal *Korean Culture of Japan*, of course.

The aim of *Korean Culture of Japan*, which Chŏng Chŏng-mun published out of his own pocket, was basically to shine new light on cultural relics and remains from ancient Korea that were visible throughout Japan— not just on Tsushima, as I described above, but also in places like Nara in the Yamato region. The goal was to help correct the still warped and misunderstood history of relations between Korea and Japan. Above all, the roundtables led by Japanese historians, archaeologists, and writers had become a kind of regular feature of the journal since its inaugural issue. They have even been collected into two volumes so far, published by a different publisher.*

* These two volumes are: *Nihon no Chōsen bunka: Zadankai*, eds. Shiba Ryōtarō, Ueda Masaaki, and Kim Tal-su (Tokyo: Chūō Kōronsha, 1972);

In this way, *Korean Culture of Japan* had no shortage of direct contributors from the Japanese side. For example, if Ri Sin-ki and I represented the Korean side, the famous historian Ueda Masayuki, who lived in Kyoto, and the writer Shida Tarō were like an advisory board for the Japanese side.**

After conferring with our collaborators Ueda and Shida, we decided to put together a roundtable called "Tsushima and Ancient Korean Culture" and set off for Tsushima right away. At least that was the plan, but we had various preparations to do beforehand. Plus, if we were going all the way to Tsushima, we really needed to spend more than just two or three nights there. So, in the end, our trip was pushed back until August 23, when summer was almost over.

Among the various preparations we had to do for the

---

and *Kodai Nihon to Chōsen: Zadankai*, eds. Shiba Ryōtarō, Ueda Masaaki, and Kim Tal-su (Tokyo: Chūō Kōronsha, 1974). [Translator]

** Ueda Masayuki (植田正行) is based on Ueda Masaaki (上田正昭, 1927–2016), a famous Japanese historian known for his work on ancient Japan, particularly in relation to Korea. Shida Tarō (志田太郎) is based on Shiba Ryōtarō (司馬遼太郎, 1923–1996), a famous Japanese writer known for his historical fiction. Kim collaborated with them many times. Ueda Masaaki traveled to Tsushima with Kim in late August 1973. [Translator]

THE TRIAL OF PAK TAL AND OTHER STORIES

trip was to enlist the help of a person named Nagano Hisataka, a local history expert who lived on Tsushima and wrote the book *The Ancient Culture of Tsushima* (Tsushima no kodai bunka).* This time, however, I wasn't much interested in hearing about local history; my mind was elsewhere. I did have some degree of interest in investigating and surveying the Korean cultural sites on Tsushima, although I had another, more pressing purpose for going there.

Most of my interest was directed toward that other purpose, and the same was true for Ri Sin-ki and Chŏng Chŏng-mun. For that reason, in preparation for our upcoming trip to Tsushima, we asked some of our friends in Tokyo and the Kansai region if they wanted to go with us, not just the roundtable participants, so when it came time to leave, we had seven or eight people in all.

When we all gathered at Osaka Airport, Ueda looked around at everyone and said, "Boy, this is a big group of people!" Perhaps he wondered why so many people wanted to go to Tsushima.

---

* Nagano Hisataka (長野久敬) is based on Nagatome Hisae (永留久惠, 1920–2015), an educator, historian, and folklorist known for his work on the local history and culture of Tsushima. [Translator]

"Tell me about it," I said, laughing. "I hear they all have something they really want to see on Tsushima."

Soon after arriving at the inn on Tsushima that evening, though, Ueda quickly seemed to realize why everyone had come all the way here. For he knew all too well what kind of relationship we had with the divided Korean Peninsula.

By the time the boat arrived at Izuhara on Tsushima, it was already past eight at night, so we went straight to our inn. The local history expert Nagano Hisataka, who was also the principal of a junior high school on Tsushima, had arranged our accommodations for us, so we invited him to join us for dinner, which turned into a kind of small party.

"Um, Nagano-*sensei*?" asked Sŏ Sam-sun, who had come from Tokyo and whose face was ruddy from the beer we were drinking. "I heard you can see Korea from Tsushima. Is that true?"

"Yes, that's true. On a clear day, you can see it quite well," Nagano replied, his voice soft and feeble but easy to understand. He truly personified the term "mild-mannered."

"Oh, really?" Sŏ Sam-sun said, glancing back at the

rest of us, who had gone quiet all of a sudden, and then continued. "Where's the best place to see it from?"

"Well, around here you can see it from Kamizaka Observatory and from Kaijin Shrine in Minemura Kisaka, where we're going tomorrow. The best place to see it, though, is probably Mt. Senbyōmaki."

"Mt. Senbyōmaki . . . what part of the island would that be?" Ri Sin-ki asked, breaking his silence and leaning forward. Then he realized something and began rifling through his travel bag behind him. He seemed to be looking for a map of Tsushima.

"That's way up north," Nagano said. While Ri Sin-ki was still searching for the map, Nagano continued: "Here's an interesting story for you. On the northern tip of the island is a place called Mt. Kōrai. Now it's a base for the Self-Defense Forces, but if you look through one of their state-of-the-art telescopes, you can supposedly see Korea clearly enough to spot the legs on chickens pecking for food in the yards of farmhouses near Pusan."

"Wow, that's amazing!"

"No way . . . ."

What Nagano said also meant that the Self-Defense Forces had installed that type of state-of-the-art telescope and were monitoring the southern Korean/South Korean port of Pusan at all times.* However, we weren't the least concerned about things like that. We were just giddy with excitement, like little children. Needless to say, that included me as well.

Just hearing the words "You can see Korea" filled my chest with complicated emotions. Even so, I tried to cover them up by raising my voice and joining in the fun, but when I looked at Sŏ Sam-sun and Kim T'ae-yŏng, who had come from Osaka, I could see their eyes brimming with tears.

Chŏng Chŏng-mun had the same look in his eyes. By that point, we didn't care anymore about investigating historical sites the next day. Instead—or at least before doing anything else—we had to go to Mt. Senbyōmaki and see if we could see Korea.

"Nagano-*san*," Ueda began, raising his lowered face. "You might not be aware of this, but these folks aren't

---

* Throughout this text, Kim often uses the term 南朝鮮・韓国 (southern Korea/South Korea), which reflects both his ethnic desire for a unified homeland (i.e., one Korean nation and people) and his recognition of the political and geographical divide between North and South Korea. While somewhat redundant and anachronistic in English, I have retained both terms in my translation. [Translator]

THE TRIAL OF PAK TAL AND OTHER STORIES

allowed to go—or go home—to South Korea or North Korea."

"Oh, I see."

Nagano, who had been beaming until that point, changed his expression slightly. Apparently, he hadn't known we were Korean.

"I believe that we Japanese are also responsible for what's happened to these folks. For that reason, would you mind first taking us to Mt. Senbyōmaki tomorrow?"

"Yes, of course. If we do that, we should leave early in the morning. Even if it's clear in the morning, it can get cloudy pretty quickly at this time of year."

Nagano still looked perplexed, but he kindly went along with Ueda's request. We had no intention whatsoever of holding Nagano and Ueda responsible as Japanese for our being stuck in Japan. Ueda's words, however, did contain a kernel of truth.

Recently, since the discovery of the Takamatsuzuka Tomb wall paintings in Asuka in the Yamato region, interest in Korea had finally begun to grow among Japanese historians and archaeologists, and many of them used this opportunity to visit southern Korea/South

Korea.* Ueda was one of them.

One night, we sat around a table with Ueda, who had just come back from South Korea, to hear stories from his trip. Before he started, Ueda first bowed his head to us and said, "I'm so sorry, everybody, for being able to go to Korea as a Japanese when you still can't."

While we were still drinking and talking up a storm, Ri Sin-ki located Mt. Senbyōmaki on his map of Tsushima. From where we were in Izuhara, it was on a cape on the western side of the island, near the northernmost point.

It was quite a long way to get up there, so if we wanted to arrive in the morning, we had to wake up at the crack of dawn. For people like me, who made a habit of staying up late and thus getting up late, that wasn't an easy task, but there was no way in hell I was going to miss this. The plan was to get up at five the next morning and leave. For breakfast, we would ask the inn to make us some rice balls, which we would eat at Mt. Senbyōmaki.

"I sure hope it's clear tomorrow . . . ."

---

* The Takamatsuzuka Tomb, an ancient burial mound containing Korean-style wall paintings, was discovered in Asuka Village (Nara Prefecture) in 1970 and excavated in 1972. [Translator]

"Me too."

Nagano and Ueda looked at each other as they said this, but then Sŏ Sam-sun said something funny, trying to make a joke. "I wonder what the weather forecast is for tomorrow. No, it's better not to know. Weather forecasts these days are too often right, so they're more trouble than they're worth."

Although Sŏ Sam-sun and Ri Sin-ki were from North Kyŏngsang Province and South Kyŏngsang Province, respectively, they both came to Japan as exchange students around August 15, 1945—in other words, just as the war was ending. Sŏ, who had come at the age of sixteen with help from his uncle in Tokyo, was now well into his forties.

Sŏ Sam-sun majored in Japanese literature at college and had a part-time job as the editor of the organ for the Korean Chamber of Commerce and Industry, which was affiliated with the General Association of Korean Residents in Japan (Chongryon, for short). For that reason, he was branded a "commie" and blacklisted by the police in his hometown, forcing even his family members there to cut off all communication with him.

Early the next morning, we left the inn in Izuhara on schedule. We headed for Mt. Senbyōmaki in the Kamiagata region, some thirty or forty miles away, in two passenger cars we'd hired through the inn to get around the island. Chŏng Chŏng-mun drove one, and Sŏ Sam-sun drove the other. Fortunately, the weather was good: there were a few clouds in the sky, but it was clear for the most part.

Since we'd arrived in Tsushima after eight the night before, this was our first chance to see the island in the light of day.

We crossed an ocean for the first time. After more than 1,000 *li*, we reached Tsuikai Province.* The ruler is called Hiku, and the deputy is called Hinamori. It is a remote island more than 400 square *li* in size. The land is covered with steep mountains and deep forests, and the roads are narrow and primitive, like animal trails.

---

* One *li* is approximately 500 meters. Tsuikai is an ancient name for Tsushima. [Translator]

This was the passage about Tsushima in the *Records of Wei: An Account of the Wa* (Wei zhi wo ren chuan), which was written near the end of the third century. Not much had changed, it seemed: the land was still "covered with steep mountains and deep forests." The blue-green mountains seemed to stretch on forever, one on top of another.

Nevertheless, I can't say that I got a very good look at the scenery. I'm sure Ri Sin-ki and the others felt the same way, but all I could think about was Mt. Senbyōmaki. *What if we're late and don't get to see the land of Korea on the horizon because of the clouds . . .* I thought, worrying myself to death.

In the end, though we weren't able to see the land of Korea after all, just as I'd feared. The following evening, as we approached a certain mountain pass, everyone got excited, saying, "Look, it's the silhouette of an island. That must be Kŏje Island!" However, it didn't look like an island to me, no matter how hard I strained my eyes.

By the time we reached the top of Mt. Senbyōmaki that day, it was a little past 8 am. We drove as fast as we could, but some sections of the roads were still "narrow and primitive, like animal trails." Plus, we had to walk the final stretch to the summit.

Perhaps because we got there late, the horizon, where Pusan should have been visible, was completely covered in thick clouds. *Aaah!* I thought, but no one said a word. We spread out and sat down by ourselves on the summit of Mt. Senbyōmaki, which was covered in waving fields of pampas grass and other wild grasses. All we could do was just sit there like that, staring out at the thick layer of clouds on the horizon.

Nevertheless, I couldn't stop my eyes from overflowing with tears. I didn't want everyone to see me crying, so I tried my best not to cry, but I couldn't help it when something welled up from deep in my heart. Soon, I was sobbing convulsively, as if I were having a coughing fit.

Even though I was a full-grown man, I was crying like a little kid. Of course, there were various thoughts and emotions behind my tears. To make a long story short, I couldn't help but feel sorry for myself for coming all the way here and not getting to see my ancestral homeland. When I happened to look up, I saw Ri Sin-ki sitting all by himself on a rocky cliff in the distance, staring toward the thick clouds blocking Pusan and repeatedly wiping tears from his eyes with his fists . . . .

This wasn't what we'd hoped for. All we saw were thick clouds hanging above the horizon, so we had no choice but to head back down the mountain. At that point, we opened the packages of rice balls we'd brought with us from the inn and had our breakfast, but the clouds showed no signs of budging the entire time.

After that, Nagano Hisataka took us around to see the ruins and relics on our original itinerary, beginning with a Gaya-style burial mound in Hitakatsu on the northeastern coast of the island, where some bronze halberds and other examples of so-called Yayoi culture had been unearthed. Gaya, also called Gara, was the name of a confederacy of small states in ancient southern Korea. The fact that the burial mound was built in the Gaya style could only mean one thing: it was a tomb for people who had moved here from the Korean state of Gaya.

Moreover, the person who had discovered the burial mound, which was built on top of a small hill overlooking the port and village of Hitakatsu, was evidently a young Korean boy named Kim so-and-so who had attended the elementary school in Hitakatsu. It was interesting to be able to feel a certain kinship with those ancient ruins, and

Ueda Masayuki even said, "It's like a connection through time," but most of them didn't really interest me.

I even started to think things like: *If that's what we were looking for, we didn't have to come all the way to Tsushima; there are plenty of sites like this in mainland Japan.* It was as if I were looking for some kind of pretext for a fight.

After that, we went on to Minemura, which is in the middle of the long and narrow island of Tsushima. There, we visited Kaijin Shrine in Kisaka, a large old shrine known as the Chief Shrine of Tsushima Province. We went there to see some of their Shilla Buddhas and Koryŏ celadon from ancient Korea, but I found myself disappointed yet again.

It's not that I was unimpressed by the Shilla Buddhas or the Koryŏ celadon at the shrine. They were all wonderful, especially the bronze Standing Nyorai (Tathāgata), which was thought to be from around the eighth century and was one of the most superb Shilla Buddhas I'd ever seen.

While I'm at it, I might add that this shrine also used to have a temple bell that was brought over from Shilla. Nagano Hisataka writes about that in his book *The*

Ancient Culture of Tsushima:

> The *Tsushima Shrine Gazetteer* [Taishū jinja shi]
> states, "There is a bell tower in front of the Hachiman
> Shrine Office with a precious bell hanging in it." Also,
> a dedication on a rafter in the bell tower is dated to the
> 14th year of the Keichō era [1609]. The inscription on this
> bell was dated to the 4th year of the Dazhong era (the era
> name of the Xuanzong Emperor of the Tang Dynasty,
> 854) and mentioned that the bell had been made in
> Shilla. The text of the inscription is recorded in *Records
> of Tsushima* [Tsushima kiji], but the bell no longer
> exists. During the separation of Shintō and Buddhism
> in the early years of the Meiji era [1868–1912], the bell
> tower was torn down and the bell was demolished and
> discarded. Had it survived, it would have become quite a
> national treasure.

What a pity, I thought, but this story didn't really
pique my interest either. I was more interested in seeing
Korea than reading about it. Supposedly, if you came to
Kaijin Shrine in the Kisaka district of Minemura, you
could see Korea from the shrine, so this time my hopes
were high.

By the time we got there in the early evening, though,

All the Way to Tsushima

the clouds on the horizon had thickened, and even the sky above Tsushima was starting to become overcast. Undeterred, we trudged up the stone steps to the hillside complex of Kaijin Shrine. From the top of the steps and from inside the grounds, we strained our eyes, trying to spot some sign of land, but all we could see were ocean and clouds.

"You could see it quite clearly yesterday," the chief priest of the shrine said after showing us the Shilla Buddhas and other objects. "But today doesn't look very promising, I'm afraid," he added, glancing toward the ocean.

"It's really unfortunate we had such bad luck today. I wonder how tomorrow will be. I hope it clears up . . . ." Nagano said with a truly sorrowful look on his face, as though he felt responsible.

We stayed at an inn in Minemura that night, and everyone got a little rowdy while drinking at dinner. Sŏ Sam-sun got drunk and ended up arguing over something minor with one of Nagano's friends, a local history expert who had come all the way to Minemura that night just to see us.

This local history expert was the person who had

arranged a boat for us to see the Korean-style fortress on Asō Bay the next day, but he never showed up the next morning, perhaps because of what had happened the night before. To make matters worse, Tsushima was completely overcast the next morning and remained so throughout the day.

Feeling as gloomy as the overcast sky, we walked around the ruins of the Korean-style fortress, Kaneda Castle, which was hard to reach unless you approached it from the bay. On a clear day, apparently, you could see Korea from Asō Bay as well, but all we could see were clouds.

Then we went further south to Takutsutama Shrine in Tsutsu, the southernmost point in the Shimoagata region.* From there, we visited a mountain shrine called "Tentō-sama" (The Sun God), which was made of stacked stones. This meant we'd traversed almost the entire length of the island of Tsushima since the previous day. When we made it to this part of the island, we finally cheered up a little.

We weren't happy just because this stone shrine called

---

* Takutsutama Shrine (多久頭魂神社) is also pronounced Takuzudama Shrine. [Translator]

All the Way to Tsushima

"Tentō-sama" was exactly like the ones you find in Korea. Here, we also picked burrs from the chestnut trees by the side of the mountain road. Hooting and hollering like little kids again, we crushed the burrs with our feet, taking out the nuts and popping them into our mouths.

Since it was summer, the chestnut burrs were still green, but in order to crush the burrs and use your fingernails to peel off the outer skin and the soft, astringent skin surrounding the nut inside, you needed the kind of technique that can only be learned from a young age. The most skilled among us was Sŏ Samsun, who was raised in a mountain village in North Kyŏngsang Province.

In other words, we all used to peel chestnuts like this when we were growing up in Korea, so Chŏng Chŏngmun was the worst at it, even though he was from the same mountain village in North Kyŏngsang as Sŏ Samsun. You see, he moved to Kyoto when he was six, so he hadn't done it very much back in Korea.

By the time we made it all the way to Daikō-ji Temple in Kunehama, it was already early evening, so we decided to head back to Izuhara after that. At Daikō-ji Temple, we were shown some Koryŏ Buddhas from Korea, such as a cute bronze statue of Shaka (Shakyamuni) at Birth—who seemed to proclaim, "I alone am worthy of honor," even as an infant—and a similar Seated Shaka Nyorai (Buddha Shakyamuni). When we left, we happened to notice that the sky was starting to clear up.

We had to cross a number of mountains on our way back to Izuhara, so we looked at each other and thought, *Maybe we can see Korea from one of those mountains* . . . . Our first glimpse came just after we passed Kune Inaka, as we were approaching one of the mountain passes.

The people in the car ahead of us, driven by Sŏ Sam-sun, had all gotten out and were screaming and shouting, pointing at something across the ocean. They claimed they could see the silhouette of Kŏje Island in the distance.

"That's an island, alright. I don't know if it's Kŏje Island, but it's definitely a Korean island," Ueda said to me, pointing in that direction and getting a little excited himself.

I looked, too, of course. There were still some clouds on the horizon, catching the last rays of the setting sun. If you looked carefully, you could see a kind of black dot under those sunset-colored clouds, like the footprint of a bird.

No matter how hard I looked, though, that was all I could see. I kept quiet, not wanting to rain on everyone's parade, but I couldn't help but think, *That's it?* Sŏ Sam-sun was jumping for joy, but it seemed to me he was doing it on purpose, as though he were consciously trying to brighten the mood or cheer everyone up.

"What do you think? Is that an island? Is it Kŏje Island?" I asked Nagano, who was standing next to me. If it was Kŏje Island, I wanted to convince myself that it was. I'm sure that's why I asked him for his opinion.

"Well, it might be, but it doesn't usually look like that. It's much clearer. You can see the mountains around Pusan much more clearly. If you want, how about coming back another time during the fall?"

"When in the fall . . . ?"

"Toward the end of October or early November. It's still summer right now, so it's often cloudy, but later in the fall, when high pressure from the continent builds up, Korea and Tsushima get long stretches of clear days."

Nagano had an utterly consolatory look on his face, and he sounded as if he were about to cry. Perhaps it was the tone of his voice that persuaded me to come back.

"Allllrightee then," I yelled toward the ocean. "I'm

comin' back in the fall! And when I do, I'm gonna come see you no matter what it takes!"

Come to think of it, it was a pretty childish thing to say, but I was totally serious when I said it. That's why I said it again to Chŏng Chŏng-mun, Ri Sin-ki, and the others on the boat as we left Izuhara the next morning.

But something odd happened. After I returned to Tokyo, the days turned into weeks, and before I knew it, the memory of what I'd felt on Tsushima began to fade away. One reason was because I was so busy with work each day. Two months flew by, and then it was late October, the time of year Nagano had invited me to come back.

But all I thought was: *Hmm, it's already fall. Didn't I say I was gonna go back to Tsushima around now?* Fall went by in the blink of an eye. And winter, too.

Meanwhile, the next thing I knew, summer rolled around again, and then fall. I still thought about Tsushima from time to time when something reminded me of it, but for the most part I'd completely forgotten about it.

One day, Ri Sin-ki asked me, "Whaddya say? It's already October, but shall we find some time to go to

All the Way to Tsushima

Tsushima? This time, I want to check out the ruins of the place where the Korean envoys stayed on their way to the shogunate in Edo . . . ."

"Oh yeah, Tsushima. I'd love to go. But if we go, we really need to stay for at least five or six days. We can't come back this time without seeing Korea."

When we left Tsushima the first time, I'd said something like, "The next time I come to Tsushima, I want to spend more time here. Maybe I'll stay near Mt. Senbyōmaki and do some fishing . . . ." At the time, I'd really meant it.

"But it's already October, so I don't think we'll have any problems like last time. Plus, if you wanted to go to Korea, you couldn't go for just five or six days."

"If you wanted to go to Korea" was a weird argument to make, but I nodded and said, "Yeah, I see what you mean. Should we just bite the bullet and go?"

Once we decided to go, I was the one who got fired up about it again. I immediately told Chŏng Chŏng-mun in Kyoto, and he said he'd find a way to go with us somehow.

This time, though, we decided to limit our group to only three or four people. Chŏng Chŏng-mun said that if we could go there and accomplish our goal in one day, it

would be fine to have a bigger group, but if we weren't able
to do that, it would be an imposition on the other people
and more trouble for us.

He was right. Thus, I only told Sǒ Sam-sun, who lived
nearby, that we were planning to go to Tsushima. I didn't
want him to feel left out since he lived so close to us, but
he said, "No, I'm good. I learned my lesson the first time.
You all go without me." After he said this, he smoothly
rubbed his outstretched palm down his crinkled face. He
often did that when he was confused about what to do.

So, in the end, it was just the three of us who went to
Tsushima on this second trip. After coordinating our
schedules, we decided to leave from Kyoto on October 21.

This was how Ri Sin-ki, Chǒng Chǒng-mun, and
I ended up back at the tiny harbor on Iki, waiting for
the boat to Tsushima again. I wrote earlier about what
we did to pass the time, but eventually we boarded the
boat bound for Tsushima from Fukuoka. On the way in,
it crossed paths with the boat heading in the opposite
direction. Thinking I would splurge a little this time,
I bought deluxe tickets for the three of us. One reason
was because the boat still had things like "first class" and

All the Way to Tsushima

"deluxe class." Once we boarded, though, we saw there was an empty deluxe suite right in front of our deluxe cabin. In that case, we figured, we might as well go all out, so we went into the deluxe suite.

We sat down on the chaise lounge and the sofa, respectively, and looked around the room. The deluxe suite was quite spacious, with a television in one corner and even two beds against the far wall. When the boat left port, a cabin steward in a white uniform came by. We paid him the fare difference and added a tip.

Now that we'd come this far, there was no turning back, even if one of us had second thoughts. We had no choice but to stay on this boat headed straight to Tsushima.

Ri Sin-ki stood up and left. Just as I was wondering where he'd gone, he came back with an armful of canned beers from the snack bar. Everything was going smoothly so far. In about two more hours, we would arrive in Tsushima.

"Still, I keep thinking . . ." Chǒng Chǒng-mun said as he took a canned beer from the table and drank it. "Wouldn't it be nice if we were on a boat going to Korea, not Tsushima? Man, how I'd love to drink like this on that boat or, better yet, back home in Korea."

"Yeah, I agree. But don't say stuff like that—it makes me homesick."

"That reminds me of An Kil-ŏn," Ri Sin-ki said. "Once, when we were out drinking together, he said this to me. 'If I went home to Korea,' he said, 'I wouldn't want to go to a cabaret or a nightclub even if someone asked me to. If I went to Seoul, I'd rather go for a drink in a dingy *makgeolli jib* on the back streets of Chongno or somewhere. If I did that, I could die a happy man right then and there.'"*

An Kil-ŏn was a historian, like Ri Sin-ki, who lectured at a certain university in Osaka. Chŏng Chŏng-mun and I both knew him well, but I'd never heard him say anything like that before.

"Really? We should have asked him to come with us."

"No, no," Ri Sin-ki said, shaking his head. "That's not a good idea. I did think about asking him last time, but it's better not to say anything to him."

"Oh, I see. Well, some people are like that."

I recalled Sŏ Sam-sun saying "I learned my lesson

---

* *Makgeolli jib* is a Korean term for a bar or stall that serves *makgeolli*, a cloudy Korean rice wine similar to *t'akchu*. [Translator]

All the Way to Tsushima

the first time" and smoothly rubbing his palm down his crinkly face.

"But you were in Korea, right?" Chǒng Chǒng-mun said, looking at me. "You were a newspaper reporter in Seoul, so I bet you've had your fair share of *makgeolli* at places like that before."

"Yeah, I have. But it was during the war, so there wasn't much to begin with, and I was still only twenty-three or twenty-four at the time, so I didn't really appreciate the taste. Besides, while I may have been a newspaper reporter, I was just getting by on my low monthly salary, so I could barely afford to eat, much less drink."

"Still, you're lucky you got to go home to Korea at all. I haven't been back since they put me on the ferryboat at Pusan when I was a kid."

"Yeah, but I haven't been home in more than thirty years."

"It's been fifty years for me."

"Wow, fifty years . . . ."

I wasn't surprised by his story. I knew that he'd come to Japan when he was six and hadn't been home at all since then. But because we were now on a boat to Tsushima for the sole purpose of seeing Korea, that span of "fifty years" really hit home for me.

"Fifty years," I muttered again, looking out the window at the slowly darkening ocean. "Fifty years" was literally "half a century," but that long span of time contained the entire life history of Chŏng Chŏng-mun, who had to do everything he could just to survive as a Korean living in Japan.

Now, Chŏng Chŏng-mun was a businessman with his own real estate company. He was also a so-called man of culture who published the journal *Korean Culture of Japan* and collected old works of art from Korea on the side with his spare cash. He'd never properly finished elementary school, much less junior high. After coming with his family to live in Kyoto, he was forced to work as an apprentice in a Nishijin-ori textile shop from the age of twelve or thirteen, and he had to do a variety of other jobs as well.

Chŏng Chŏng-mun didn't have to tell me every single job he'd done in his life—I knew what they were just from looking back on my own life. Most Koreans living in Japan, especially those in their fifties, had a similar personal history. If you saw one, you saw them all.

For instance, I'm now what people would call a writer,

All the Way to Tsushima

but my earlier career was almost the same as Chǒng Chǒng-mun's. At one point, my works were chosen to be included in a certain anthology, so I was asked to write a "biographical timeline" for the appendix. As I was writing it, I looked back on my life as if seeing it anew. I, too, had been forced to work various jobs, beginning with an apprenticeship in a printing shop.

I once read that the French author Pierre Gascar, who is three years older than I, went through at least thirty different jobs when he was younger to support himself. I may not have done as many jobs as he did, but I must have done more than ten, if you count my stint as a *nattō* (fermented soybean) seller when I was a kid.

Later, I became a newspaper reporter and went back home to Korea to work in Seoul. However, I ended up "fleeing Seoul and returning to Japan," as I wrote in my biographical timeline. Then the Pacific War ended, and Japan became "postwar" while Korea became "liberated." Here is what my biographical timeline says about my life that year:

THE TRIAL OF PAK TAL AND OTHER STORIES

1945   25 years old

> In June, he leaves K Newspaper Company, where
> he had been working (since returning to Japan), after
> it goes up in flames during an air raid. In August, the
> Pacific War ends. Soon thereafter, he participates in the
> formation of the ethnic organization Chōren (League of
> Koreans in Japan). He is full of energy and vitality.

Leaving aside the question of how I was "full of energy
and vitality" back then, my life took many twists and
turns after that, but I still kept moving forward on the
path I'd chosen and eventually became a professional
literary writer.

During that time, though, the supposedly independent
country of Korea was divided by the two superpowers,
the United States and the Soviet Union, and drawn
into a vortex of international politics no one could have
anticipated. Chŏng Chŏng-mun, Ri Sin-ki, and I were
originally from southern Korea/South Korea, where more
than ninety-seven percent of Koreans living in Japan are
from. At first, South Korea was ruled by the American-
backed dictator Syngman Rhee, but after his regime was
toppled, it became a military dictatorship under the rule

of Park Chung-hee, who was supported by the United States and the newly resurgent Japan.

That was my first introduction to how politics really works, but whether I liked it or not, I had to choose my own political perspective vis-à-vis these issues. My "political perspective" was none other than my own ethnic position as a Korean, which I'd been deprived of.

Even so, I found myself ostracized by the foreign-backed dictatorship in South Korea. Before I knew it, I'd become an exile, an outcast from my hometown and my homeland.

It was the same for Chŏng Chŏng-mun, who experienced the end of the war at an airfield construction site he'd been sent to after being drafted. Like me, he was "full of energy and vitality," so he spent many years laying the foundations for his current career as a businessman. At the same time, he also became a leader of the Korean Chamber of Commerce and Industry, which was affiliated with the pro-North Korean group Chongryon—an offshoot of Chōren, the group I'd helped form. He ran around trying to build ethnic schools to provide ethnic education for Korean children living in Japan.

This project took on an even greater urgency for him

THE TRIAL OF PAK TAL AND OTHER STORIES

precisely because he'd never been able to receive that kind
of formal education. He, too, was excluded and shut out
from his hometown and his homeland for doing this,
though.

Ri Sin-ki, the youngest among us by almost ten years,
followed a different path in life, but he ended up in the
same place as us. As I briefly touched upon earlier, he
graduated from a junior high school in Pusan and came
to Japan to study right before the Pacific War ended.

After Japan became "postwar" and Korea became
"liberated," he became a teacher at an ethnic school in
Tokyo. On the side, he attended a certain university all
the way through graduate school, majoring in history and
archaeology. This must have required a great deal of effort
on his part.

His research, which reconsidered how Japanese
historians and archaeologists have overlooked Japan's
relationship with Korea until now, was receiving
considerable attention from both the academic world
and the reading public in Japan. Sure enough, though, he
became an exile and an outcast, too, for being a teacher
at an ethnic school affiliated with Chongryon. He hadn't
been back to his hometown and his homeland for more

than thirty years either.

"Hahaha . . . time flies, huh?" I laughed loudly as I opened another can of beer. "That means we're getting older too. At this rate, we'll be a bunch of old geezers in no time."

"You got that right," Chŏng Chŏng-mun replied, not even cracking a smile. "The past fifty years have just been crazy. For twenty years before and during the war, and thirty years since then, I've been so focused on stuff here that I haven't even had time to think about my hometown."

"It's the same for all of us. I went to Seoul for about a year, but I never went back to my hometown while I was there. I had more important things to worry about."

"I guess that means we're old after all. You might laugh at me for saying this, but they often have programs like *Memorable Hits of the Shōwa Era* or whatever on TV, right? The singers who appear on those programs used to be so young and gorgeous back in the day, but now when I see the wrinkles on their faces, I think to myself, *Ahh, those days are long gone.*"

"I guess what you mean is that we're all going to die sooner or later, just some of us sooner rather than later."

"Exactly. Maybe that's why I often remember things from my childhood these days, although I left Korea when I was six and haven't been back since, so my memories are pretty vague. But I remember some things really well, like a small river that ran through our *tongnae*.* We used to play in the water a lot, splashing each other. If you follow this river downstream, it turns into the much bigger Naktong River. I have this ridiculously clear image in my mind of the Naktong River glittering in the evening sun, probably because I've been thinking about it so much recently."

"Ah, the Naktong River. I bet it's pretty up there."

Ri Sin-ki and I were born near Masan, in South Kyŏngsang Province, not in North Kyŏngsang Province, where the Naktong River starts. To get to Masan, you take the train from Pusan and switch to a local line at a place called Samnangjin. From Samnangjin, the train immediately crosses an iron bridge. The river underneath is the Naktong River.

As a result, I only got to see the Naktong River when I crossed that bridge as a child, so I didn't know much

---

* *Tongnae* is a Korean term meaning "village" or "neighborhood." [Translator]

about it. However, I'd heard a lot about it, not just from Chŏng Chŏng-mun but also from Sŏ Sam-sun, whose hometown was nearby. The Naktong River was no doubt a "mother river" to them.

"I grew up in Kimhae, on the lower reaches of the Naktong River, so we always used to go swimming there," Ri Sin-ki chimed in from the side. For some reason, he'd been listening to our conversation silently until that point.

"Oh, that's right."

I knew that the Naktong River, which begins where the Sopaek Mountains split off to the southwest from the T'aebaek Mountains, was a large river running north to south through Yŏngnam (the generic name for North and South Kyŏngsang Provinces), but I'd completely forgotten where it flowed on its way to the ocean.

"Naktong River . . . Just saying those two words always makes me tear up inside, like a little kid or something. Sometimes I feel like I can't take it anymore."

Perhaps to drown his sorrows, Chŏng Chŏng-mun took a can of beer from the table and drank it. It was the can I'd been drinking from. Without saying anything, I took his beer and drank it.

"So how does it feel, being on the Genkai Sea again?"

Ri Sin-ki asked, trying to steer the conversation in a different direction. "I know this guy who makes a face like he's having an allergic reaction whenever he hears the words 'Genkai Sea.'"

"Ahh, the Genkai Sea," I said. "There's something kind of nostalgic about it now, but I can imagine some people would become allergic to thinking about that ferryboat after all these years."

In Japan, the word for the Genkai Sea (玄海灘) was now written with a different second character (玄界灘), but for us Koreans living in Japan, it was always written Hyŏnhaet'an (玄海灘), not Hyŏn'gyet'an (玄界灘). Also, for us Koreans living in Japan, the Genkai Sea was always tied to memories of the Shimonoseki–Pusan ferryboat and the Hakata–Pusan ferryboat, so it was impossible for anyone to forget it.

Maybe it was just my imagination, or maybe it was because we were approaching the coast of Tsushima, but our boat began to rock quite a bit. This was nothing, though, compared to the pitching and rolling of the ferryboat when it crossed the Genkai Sea.

"I was still a young boy when I made the crossing, and it was right before the end of the war, so it wasn't too bad for me, but I hear that everyone had rough experiences on the ferryboat," Ri Sin-ki said.

"You mean the ideological screenings, right? I don't even want to think about them again—and everything else we had to go through—but they did force us to become aware of many things. In that sense, they were like a good example of what not to do. I was pretty clueless back then, perhaps because I grew up mostly in Japan. It was only from those undercover detectives who conducted the ideological screenings that I learned there were—or apparently were, I should say—various forms of independence movements and revolutionary movements even during the war."

"That's why my friend with the allergy said that if you made two or three round trips across the Genkai Sea, that was enough to make you realize you were Korean, whether you wanted to or not."

"That's true, but it wasn't very pleasant. Everybody had warned me about the ideological screenings, so I planned to avoid bringing anything that might get me in trouble, but I accidentally brought along a paperback copy of *Anna Karenina*."

"Was that not allowed?"

"Of course not. The author, Tolstoy, was Russian, which meant he was a Soviet worker-farmer in their eyes."

"Wow, really? Did you get hit, like everybody else did? My friend with the allergy says everybody got hit at least once or twice . . . ."

"I didn't get hit that time, but the next time I got on, one of the detectives said I gave him a defiant look, so he hit me. It happened so suddenly that the blood gushed out of my nose and splattered on his clothes. So he hit me again."

"You must have given him one hell of a look," Ri Sin-ki laughed. There was nothing you could do but laugh about it now.

"I was young, after all. Plus, I was an ambitious newspaper reporter, so I thought pretty highly of myself."

"Still . . ." Chŏng Chŏng-mun said, sitting across from us. "Like I said before, you're lucky you got to go home to Korea at all."

"Yeah, I suppose . . . ."

"It still bugs me, though," Chŏng Chŏng-mun continued. "On August 15, 1945—8.15, as they call it in Korea—we were liberated from colonial rule, right? Right?"

"Officially, anyway."

I knew what Chŏng Chŏng-mun was going to say next, so I gave him a half-hearted response and looked away. The boat was rocking pretty hard now. Perhaps the wind had kicked up.

"And yet," Chŏng Chŏng-mun continued. "Even during the colonial period, we were still able to go back and visit our hometown and our homeland, although we sometimes got roughed up a bit. But now we can't go home at all. Now you tell me: which do you think is better?"

There was no way Ri Sin-ki or I could answer that. Of course, Chŏng Chŏng-mun hadn't been looking for an answer.

"And it's not just us, either. You can say the same thing about the people in our native land, which has been divided in two," Ri Sin-ki said, as though talking to himself. He stood up, struggling to keep his balance as the boat lurched to one side. He walked over toward the beds, but judging from the pallid look on his face, he appeared to be seasick.

When I saw Ri Sin-ki's face, I started to feel a little sick myself, so I lay down on the chaise lounge after he left.

Chŏng Chŏng-mun was sitting on the sofa resignedly, but eventually he stretched out his legs and lay down on his back, too.

As in the previous year, we arrived at Tsushima just after 8 pm. We all walked down the gangway in high spirits, no longer queasy. We decided to visit the same inn we'd stayed at the previous year and ask if they could put us up for the night.

The next morning, we set out in a passenger car hired through the inn and driven by Chŏng Chŏng-mun, just as in the previous year. In other respects, though, things were different from the previous year. Not only did we take it easy in the morning and not leave the inn until after 9 am, but we were completely calm about the overcast sky above Tsushima that day.

Ri Sin-ki asked if we should contact Nagano Hisataka, the local historian who had taken care of us the first time we came to Tsushima, but we decided against it. Not only did we feel bad about imposing on him again, but we also thought he might become a burden on us. In short, we wanted to be free to explore Tsushima on our own.

All we had to do that day was make it to Sasuna, near

All the Way to Tsushima

Mt. Senbyōmaki, by nightfall. Not only was Sasuna the closest place to Mt. Senbyōmaki with an inn, but it was also where the Korean envoys made landfall on their way to the shogunate in Edo. Ri Sin-ki was researching this topic, so he wanted to stay there.

Thus, all we had to do was stay at the inn in Sasuna and wait a day or two for the weather to clear. While we were waiting, Chŏng Chŏng-mun and I could either join Ri Sin-ki and explore where the Korean envoys had made landfall, or we could drop our lines in the ocean and try to catch some fish. I did have some unfinished work that was hanging over my head, but I decided to think about it as little as possible while I was on Tsushima.

In a more relaxed frame of mind this time, we rode in the passenger car toward the town of Izuhara, which reminded us of Korea with its many houses surrounded by stone walls. Sasuna was only a couple hours by car from Izuhara, so we had more than half a day to spare. I don't remember who suggested it, but we somehow found ourselves heading toward Kamizaka Observatory, northwest of Izuhara.

The observatory was on top of a mountain that had been turned into a park. When we climbed to the top

THE TRIAL OF PAK TAL AND OTHER STORIES

of the iron turret, we found a direction plaque showing the various places you could see from the observatory, including an arrow pointing to South Korea. However, it was overcast that day, so there was no way you could see Korea. But we weren't the least bit worried.

"I'm pretty sure the former Tsushima garrison was located somewhere around here, though not in Izuhara. Shall we go take a look?" Ri Sin-ki said as we climbed down from the observatory.

"You mean the place where Ch'oe Ik-hyŏn was held?" I asked. Actually, I'd been thinking the exact same thing.

"Yes, that's right. The site of the former Tsushima garrison might now be a base for the Self-Defense Forces."

"Who's Ch'oe Ik-hyŏn?" Chŏng Chŏng-mun asked. It wasn't surprising that he didn't know who Ch'oe Ik-hyŏn was. I only knew because I happened to be writing a work set during that time period, so I'd had to do some research on him. Ch'oe Ik-hyŏn might be called the "last loyal retainer" of the Joseon Dynasty.

The Joseon Dynasty came to an end as a result of Japan's so-called annexation of Korea in 1910. However, the stage had been set for this annexation five years earlier with the signing of the Japan–Korea Treaty of 1905, also known as the Eulsa Protection Treaty.

Although the Eulsa Protection Treaty was forced on Korea by the new imperial power of Japan and its army, which had just defeated Russia in the Russo-Japanese War, the five ministers who signed it—including Pak Che-sun and Yi Wan-yong—were later branded the "Five Traitors." This term "Five Traitors," by the way, is still alive and well today under the military dictatorship of Park Chung-hee. In response to these actions of the Japanese army and the "Five Traitors," multiple "righteous armies" began fighting in Korea at the same time.

Ch'oe Ik-hyŏn, a former junior councillor (an imperial appointee to the State Council of Joseon), was a member of one of these "righteous armies." He voiced strong opposition to the Eulsa Protection Treaty, first by issuing his famous "Letter of Appeal" to the Korean emperor.* This was noted in Japanese records as well. For example, Aoyagi Nanmei's book *Korean History and Historic Sites* (Chōsen shiwa to shiseki) includes a fairly detailed

---

* Ch'oe's appeal has been translated into English as "Ch'oe Ikhyŏn: An Appeal to Arms" in *Sources of Korean Tradition Volume 2: From the Sixteenth to the Twentieth Centuries*, eds. Yŏng-ho Ch'oe, Peter H. Lee, and Wm. Theodore de Bary (New York: Columbia University Press, 2000) 292–294. [Translator]

description of it in a chapter entitled "Ch'oe Ik-hyŏn: The Sole Loyal Retainer of the Late Korean Empire":

> With the signing of the Japan–Korea Treaty of 1905, the entire capital—elites and commoners alike—was sent into an uproar, with people calling the five ministers traitors to the nation and exhibiting a state of unrest marked by extreme anger and indignation. Furthermore, one hundred government officials, led by former Privy Councillor Cho Pyŏng-se and others, made a report to the throne, asking that the five ministers be punished, and sent letters to the diplomatic envoys from each country requesting joint negotiations, but none of those countries' envoys responded.
>
> Former Envoy to Russia and Cabinet Minister Min Yŏng-hwan, realizing there was nothing he could do to stop the treaty from being ratified, committed suicide, as did Cho Pyŏng-se, followed by Deputy Minister Hong Man-sik and Envoy to England Yi Han-ŭng.

Amidst this situation, Ch'oe Ik-hyŏn issued his stinging "Letter of Appeal," which Aoyagi Nanmei describes as follows:

> Prior to this, Ch'oe Ik-hyŏn had gone home to

Chŏngsan in Hosŏ, where he was passionately teaching a group of students while still worrying about the current state of affairs. When he learned that the new treaty had been signed and the political world in Hanseong [Seoul] was in chaos, he was enraged. He composed an appeal to Emperor Gojong, urging him to kill the five ministers, and delivered this to the emperor's palace by secret messenger. The preface to his appeal begins:

> In my humble opinion, every era has its share of rebels and traitors, but none so deplorable as Foreign Affairs Minister Pak Che-sun, Interior Minister Ri Chi-yong, Army Minister Ri Kŭn-t'aek, Education Minister Yi Wan-yong, and Agriculture, Commerce, and Industry Minister Cho Chung-hyŏn, who recently took matters into their own hands and signed an agreement ceding control of our diplomatic affairs.* In advance of this signing, the Japanese envoys had already come here for the sake of establishing a new agreement, so there is no way our government could not have known about this. Seeing that they already knew about this and did not outline it fully to the

---

* Cho Chung-hyŏn (趙重顯) is a misspelling of Kwŏn Chung-hyŏn (權重顯). [Translator]

THE TRIAL OF PAK TAL AND OTHER STORIES

country or tell the people that many would surely perish—which is to say, the way that they behaved so cowardly by setting up a meeting in the middle of the night, when no one would notice—there can be little doubt that they were intending to betray the country.

This is just the beginning of the preface to Ch'oe Ik-hyŏn's "Letter of Appeal." There is no point in examining it fully here, but it is worth noting that he was already over seventy years old when he wrote it. Nonetheless, Ch'oe Ik-hyŏn made numerous such "appeals" and issued multiple manifestos. Eventually, in June 1906, he conspired with Lim Pyŏng-ch'an, the former constable of the Taein district, to form a "righteous army" of more than a hundred people in Taein, in North Chŏlla Province.

"Righteous armies" are what we now call guerillas. The *Records on the Subjugation of Korean Rebels* (Chōsen bōto tōbatsu shi), compiled by the Japanese Korean Garrison Army Headquarters, which fought bitterly against the "righteous armies," contains detailed information about them. The final section regarding Ch'oe Ik-hyŏn goes as follows:

All the Way to Tsushima

When the rebels staged an uprising in the Taein district, the Chŏnju Military Police Advisory Branch dispatched police officers to capture the leaders of the rebellion, but instead they were encircled by the rebels and found themselves in dire straits. By this point, the rebels had advanced to Sunch'ang from the direction of Tongpok and Koksŏng, so the police took advantage of this opportunity to send in subjugation units from Namwŏn and Chŏnju on June 11. They cut off the main roads from all three directions—Chŏnju, Namwŏn, and Kwangju—and surrounded Sunch'ang. After half a day of fighting, the rebels finally gave in, and the two leaders Ch'oe and Lim surrendered along with their followers.

On June 16, our soldiers transferred Ch'oe and his followers to Keijō [Seoul]. On August 4, Ch'oe Ik-hyŏn was sentenced to three years in prison and Lim Pyŏng-ch'an was sentenced to two years in prison, and their respective followers were punished. Ch'oe was sent to Tsushima to serve out his sentence. In January of Meiji 40 [1907], he died from an illness in exile.

It says, "he died from an illness in exile," but that's not what actually happened. Ch'oe Ik-hyŏn, who was exiled to the Japanese territory of Tsushima, left behind a stinging

"Posthumous Appeal," which he sent to the Korean emperor. According to Aoyagi Nanmei's chapter on Ch'oe Ik-hyŏn in *Korean History and Historic Sites*, the appeal read:

> I, Your loyal subject Ch'oe Ik-hyŏn, am facing death in the Tsushima garrison in Japan. I bow twice toward the west and offer a prayer to Your Majesty. As I humbly recall, I already outlined my plans to raise a righteous army in an appeal to Your Majesty at the beginning of this whole affair in the intercalary fourth month [June] of this year. Although I still have no way of knowing whether or not my original appeal reached Your Majesty, my efforts to raise a righteous army were in vain. Eventually, I surrendered and was taken prisoner. On the eighth day of the seventh month [August], I was transferred to the Japanese island of Tsushima. Indeed, I am imprisoned in the so-called Tsushima garrison. It is clear to me that there is no hope of making it out of here alive; I shall most certainly die here. While the Japanese bandits' emotions are still unfathomable to me, I will never stop until I kill them.

> Let me add one more thought, if I may. Since coming to this island, everything I have been given—whether it be a spoonful of rice or a gulp of water—has come from

the hands of the Japanese bandits. Even if I do not kill them, I cannot stomach the thought of eating their food any longer, so I have finally resolved to go on a hunger strike.

I am seventy-four years old. Why should I begrudge death? The only thing I regret is not being able to fight the traitors and not being able to overthrow the Japanese invasion. Our sovereignty has yet to be reclaimed, and our territory has yet to be returned. The righteous way of 4,000 years of Chinese cultural heritage has been reduced to a pile of manure, and it cannot be rescued. The children of the former kings of Korea have become like fish on the chopping block, and they cannot be saved. I may die, but I will never be able to rest in peace.

Even as he faced death in prison, he was determined not to go down without a fight. In other words, Ch'oe Ik-hyŏn refused to accept any food or drink "from the hands of the Japanese bandits" and starved himself to death.

"Resentment runs deep on this island of Tsushima, doesn't it? Not only in the distant past, but also in more recent times," Chŏng Chŏng-mun said, driving the car down a hill. "We Koreans living in Japan are like the

THE TRIAL OF PAK TAL AND OTHER STORIES

offspring of that resentment."

"When you put it like that, I guess you're right," I nodded. Then I suddenly changed my mind and said, "By the way, let's skip the Tsushima garrison ruins today."

"Good idea," Ri Sin-ki quickly agreed. "Even if we went, it's not like there's anything left to see."

"You're probably right. Let's take it easy for once this time," Chŏng Chŏng-mun added.

So, we took the road that went back to Izuhara and headed toward Kashine, where we visited Hōsei-ji Temple. We hadn't had time to go there on our previous visit.

At that small temple tucked away in a ravine, we were shown a Kŏryo Buddha. Afterward, we ate persimmons from a tree inside the temple grounds, plucking them from the branches with a bamboo pole as we used to do when we were kids. The head priest's wife, who was complaining that her only son had run off to Tokyo and wouldn't come home to take over the temple, watched us with curiosity. She even picked some persimmons herself and offered them to us.

Eating those persimmons melted all our cares away. Next, we drove through Kechi—where the new Tsushima

Airport was under construction—and Ōfunakoshi on our way to Kofunakoshi. By the time we got there, it was already late in the afternoon.

We stopped in Kofunakoshi not only because it was on the way to Sasuna, but also because the Korean envoys had come ashore here as well. Actually, the envoys landed at various places throughout Tsushima, not just Sasuna, and stayed there for many nights before finally heading to Iki. Here, however, something happened that completely spoiled the carefree mood we'd maintained until that point.

There was a temple in Kofunakoshi called Bairin-ji Temple, which held a Kŏryo Tripitaka with historical ties to the envoys. Everything would have been fine had we just left after seeing the sutra, but there was a snazzy new agricultural cooperative office next to the temple. I doubt he was attracted by the building's fancy design, but Chŏng Chŏng-mun went inside and borrowed the phone to let his family in Kyoto know where he was.

Chŏng Chŏng-mun often did that when we traveled together, so I didn't think twice about it. However, when he came out with a glum look on his face, he said to me and Ri Sin-ki, "There aren't any more boats today, so I can't leave tonight, but I have to go back to Kyoto tomorrow."

"What happened? What time tomorrow . . . ?"

There were only two boats a day from Izuhara to Fukuoka. The first was at 8:30 am, and the second was at 3 pm. If Chŏng Chŏng-mun decided to take the morning one, we'd have to backtrack to Izuhara from Kofunakoshi.

"Whichever one I take, I won't get home until late at night, so the afternoon one should be fine . . . ."

"Oh, that's good," I said, feeling relieved. If he took the afternoon boat back, we could stay in Sasuna that night and go up Mt. Senbyōmaki the next morning as planned.

"Still, I wonder if it'll clear up tomorrow," Chŏng Chŏng-mun said, looking up at the sky, which had been stubbornly overcast since that morning. "If tomorrow is as cloudy as today, I want you two to stay behind and see Korea without me."

"Yeah, but it won't be the same without you," I said, exchanging glances with Ri Sin-ki. It wouldn't be easy to stay behind by ourselves when the three of us had come here together.

Chŏng Chŏng-mun said he absolutely had to go back

to Kyoto the next day due to a business-related matter. Someone who owed him some money had defaulted on a payment, he explained, and unless he did something about it quickly, it would create a lot of problems.

Ri Sin-ki and I didn't really understand the situation, but nonetheless we tensed up and started worrying about the weather the next day. If tomorrow was as cloudy as today, then what would we do? Even if the two of us stayed behind without Chŏng Chŏng-mun, we could tell it would leave a pretty bad aftertaste between us.

Essentially, everything would be fine as long as it was clear tomorrow, if only during the morning. If the weather cooperated, that was actually better for me, since I had a ton of unfinished work waiting for me back at home.

We went straight from Kofunakoshi to Sasuna, but even after we got to Sasuna, all we could think about was the weather. Looking across the ocean, we could faintly make out the sunset, but what would tomorrow bring?

Sasuna was a small port town with a bay shaped like a long, narrow inlet. The town was once prosperous as the first port of call for the Korean envoys. Sin Yu-han, one of the envoys who came in 1719, mentioned it in his account *Records of a Sea Voyage* (Haeyurok). Ri Sin-ki had brought along a copy of this book, which included the following passage:

> Sasuura Bay is also called Sasaura Bay. It is located on the northwestern tip of Tsushima and is surrounded by mountains on all sides, resembling a giant circle. The mountains must be more than 500 feet tall. They are covered with dense forests of pine, bamboo, mandarin orange, citron, winter oak (camellia), and hemp palm. In the middle, the ocean juts in to form a circular lake where the ships all gather to anchor. [. . .]
>
> There are more than thirty homes encircling the bay. All of them have tall thatched roofs that look like upside-down bowls. The men have shaved pates and do not wear ceremonial hats. For clothing, they wear long-sleeved garments with no formal trousers. Donning swords, they sit in a semi-kneeling position. The women wear their hair in tall chignons, with sashes tied around their waists. The people are accustomed to handling boats. The land is barren and has no rice fields.

This is what Sasuna was like more than 250 years ago. But we had no time to dwell on the past. We went to our inn by the ocean and had dinner, but all we could think about was the next day's weather.

I don't know how it was down in Izuhara, but up here in Sasuna there were no evening editions of newspapers, so we had to rely on the old black-and-white TV in our room for the weather forecast. When on earth was the weather forecast, though?

Normally, I didn't pay much attention to such things, so I didn't really know when the weather forecast came on. In that regard, I was just like those people back in the old days: all I did was glance up at the sky and think to myself, *Tomorrow should be fine* or *Hmm, looks like rain.*

According to Sŏ Sam-sun, who had come with us the previous year, "weather forecasts these days are too often right," but I'd never put much faith in them. As a result, I rarely looked at them in the newspaper. When I watched TV, though, there were times when I had to listen to the weather forecast, whether I wanted to or not. There were also times when they would show a weather chart depicting the Korean Peninsula along with the Japanese archipelago.

However, when they started pointing at whorls on the chart and going into details like the amount of millibars and so forth, I had no idea what they were talking about.

That's partially because I hadn't bothered trying to understand it, but it wasn't until I came to Tsushima that I finally became a little better informed about weather forecasting.

Ri Sin-ki helped explain it to me as we looked at the general weather chart that finally appeared on the TV in our room at about ten o'clock. According to him, the whorl spinning and spreading out over the Korean Peninsula and the Liaodong Peninsula was called a high-pressure system building up from the continent. The closer it came to the Japanese archipelago, the greater our chances were for clear weather.

"Therefore," Ri Sin-ki concluded, "Let's hope this part moves toward Japan. If it does, we might have clear skies tomorrow."

"We might have clear skies" was not the most reassuring way to put it, but when we watched the local forecast next, they said, "The Nagasaki Prefecture region will be partly cloudy" tomorrow with "high wind and waves, so small craft should exercise caution." That was it; they said nothing about Tsushima. With that, the weather forecast was over.

To be sure, Tsushima was technically part of Nagasaki

Prefecture. However, as you can see from looking at a map, the island was far removed from the mainland of Kyūshū. "Then why doesn't it have its own weather forecast?" I wanted to ask, but it was pointless to protest. Besides, it was absurd for someone like me, who had never placed much faith in weather forecasts to begin with, to make such a comment at this point.

"I'm sure it'll be fine," Ri Sin-ki said, as though trying to cheer himself up as well. "On the general forecast they just showed, the high-pressure ridge extended all the way to Pusan, so at least Pusan should be clear."

"So Pusan might be clear, huh?" Chŏng Chŏng-mun said, echoing Ri Sin-ki. "Relatively speaking, Tsushima is closer to Pusan than it is to Nagasaki, so if that's the case, maybe we'll be able to see it."

Even after I went to bed, though, I still couldn't stop thinking about the weather. Apparently, the wind had picked up during the night because I was awoken by the sound of the ill-fitted window rattling in its frame. When I picked up the clock next to my pillow, it showed 3 am.

I got up and opened the window, which was behind a curtain. A cold wind blew in, but I couldn't see anything outside except total darkness. Neither the ocean nor the sky was visible. Looking more carefully, I could make out just one small star glimmering alone in the pitch-black sky.

I hadn't been able to see any stars in the sky before I went to bed earlier that evening, so I took a deep breath and thought, *Hmmm, maybe that's a good sign.* Then I went back to bed and didn't wake up again until a little after 6 am.

I jumped up, brushed aside the curtain in front of the window, and flung open the window. Without even thinking, I let out a loud "Ohhhh!" The sky was a brilliant blue, not a cloud in sight.

Hearing my voice, Chŏng Chŏng-mun and Ri Sin-ki got up and rushed toward the window, nearly bumping into each other.

"Well?" I said, pointing outside with pride, as if I were trying to take credit for it.

"Nice job. It's a picture-perfect day," Chŏng Chŏng-mun said.

"The wind last night must have blown the clouds away," Ri Sin-ki said.

We decided to get ready and head out at once. We would miss breakfast, but we didn't care.

The owners of the inn were still asleep, so we quietly

slid open the front door and left without telling them. I was worried they might think the three of us had run off during the night, but they would understand once we got back.

We hopped in the car, which we'd left outside the inn, and drove toward nearby Mt. Senbyōmaki. The mountain may have been nearby, but the road to get there was full of twists and turns, so it was a fairly long drive. From beyond the mountains stretching off to the east, the beautiful, glorious sun was beginning to rise in the crystal-clear sky, painting it red.

Our car could only go halfway up the mountain. Just as in the previous year, we had to hike twenty or thirty minutes from there to the top. Standing almost 900 feet tall and dropping straight down to the ocean just past the summit, Mt. Senbyōmaki was one of the few mountains on Tsushima covered with pampas grass and other wild grasses. However, the path we climbed from where we parked was steep and narrow, much like the "animal trails" mentioned in *Records of Wei: An Account of the Wa*.

At first, the three of us climbed the path in single file, but before I knew it, I'd pushed on ahead, breaking away from the other two. The lump in my throat was so big I

THE TRIAL OF PAK TAL AND OTHER STORIES

could barely breathe. Still, I kept climbing, even as my knees became wobbly.

Finally, I reached the top. I could see Korea. The next instant, I was screaming at the top of my lungs in Korean.

"*Poyŏtta! Poinda!*" (I saw it! I see it!)

The ocean spread out before my eyes, catching the light of the morning sun. In the distance, stretching along the horizon, was a series of tall, bluish-green mountains— row upon row of them, one behind the other. In the foreground was what appeared to be an island. It was protruding in this direction, as though it had popped out from the nearby horizon.

Soon thereafter, the other two made it to the top and saw it for themselves: the land of Korea, with those unmistakable mountains.

"Ah . . ." Chŏng Chŏng-mun and Ri Sin-ki exclaimed, both their voices and their legs failing them. The three of us just stood there in a daze, unable to move or say anything.

Considering what had happened the year before, I was afraid I might start bawling my eyes out again—even more so than last time—but to my surprise, I didn't. I dabbed my eyes with my hands two or three times, but this time I felt more stunned than sad. When I looked over at Chŏng Chŏng-mun and Ri Sin-ki, they seemed to feel the same way.

"That's Chŏlyŏng Island, near Pusan, sticking out in front," Ri Sin-ki finally said, pointing at the big island. The lower part of it was made up of white cliffs, which were so clear I could almost see the spray from the waves breaking on the rocks below.

"Still, I never imagined it was this close," Chŏng Chŏng-mun said. His voice sounded as though he were still catching his breath. From where we were on the northern tip of Tsushima, it was supposedly about thirty miles to Pusan, but I couldn't help thinking the same thing. When I glanced at my wristwatch, it was just after 7 am.

After that, we roamed around the top of the mountain, staring at the mountains of Korea and Pusan—stretched out beyond the sea—for what seemed like forever. It was early in the morning on a brisk autumn day. The ocean right beneath our eyes was rough and dotted with whitecaps, so the gusts of wind that blew up from the bottom of the cliff were as cold as midwinter gales. My hands grew numb and soon felt as if they were frozen solid.

Even so, we continued wandering around the summit of Mt. Senbyōmaki. It must have been another hour or so before we finally decided to go down.

"Well, we finally saw it. Now I can say I honored my pledge to my younger brother," Ri Sin-ki said as he walked along the path through a field of pampas grass still topped with silvery plumes.

"What do you mean by that?" I asked, turning around and looking across the ocean one last time. The mountains around Pusan were still visible.

"Actually, I was afraid you might laugh at me, so I didn't tell you, but before we came to Tsushima this time, I decided to call my younger brother in Pusan," Ri Sin-ki said and began his story.

Ri Sin-ki had come to Japan after graduating from middle school in Pusan, but he'd been born and raised in Kimhae, a little farther away. His younger brother's family, however, had stayed behind in Korea and now lived in Pusan.

From time to time, Ri Sin-ki sent letters to his younger brother under an assumed name and sometimes even called him on the phone to speak with him directly. Even

All the Way to Tsushima

though Ri Sin-ki and Sŏ Sam-sun had come to Japan under similar circumstances, Sŏ's family lived in an out-of-the-way farming village in North Kyŏngsang Province, whereas Ri's family lived in the densely populated metropolis of Pusan, so it was easier for Ri to stay in touch with them.

Over the past few years, however, the situation in southern Korea/South Korea had become increasingly precarious. Events like the Kim Dae-jung Kidnapping Incident and the National Democratic Youth-Student League Incident, both of which had connections to Japan, occurred one after another.* Then, just last August, the Mun Se-gwang Incident took place in South Korea

---

* South Korean political dissident and exile Kim Dae-jung was kidnapped by the Korean Central Intelligence Agency (KCIA) from a Tokyo hotel room on August 8, 1973, for his criticism of then-president Park Chung-hee's dictatorial regime. The kidnappers eventually took him to South Korea, where he was released. The National Democratic Youth-Student League Incident occurred in April 1974, when Park Chung-hee and the KCIA cracked down on student groups and intellectuals who were rumored to be plotting a violent overthrow of the South Korean government to protest emergency decrees stemming from the 1972 Yushin Constitution. Both incidents had connections to the Zainichi Korean community, particularly the General Association of Korean Residents in Japan (Chongryon), and other individuals and organizations in Japan. [Translator]

under the military dictatorship of Park Chung-hee.*
The General Association of Korean Residents in Japan
(Chongryon) was thought to be behind it. As a result, Ri
Sin-ki's younger brother had told him not to send any
letters or make any phone calls for a while.

Nevertheless, in preparation for our second trip to
Tsushima, Ri Sin-ki decided to make an international
phone call to his younger brother in Pusan. Actually,
an international phone call wasn't much different than
calling from Tokyo to somewhere in Kyūshū.

"When I told him I was coming," Ri Sin-ki continued,
"he asked me when I'd be looking at Pusan from
Tsushima. So I said if the weather was clear, it would
probably be on the morning of the 22nd, and if not, then
probably on the 23rd or the 24th. When I told him that,
my brother said he'd be looking toward Tsushima from
Pusan on those days, too."

"Oh, really? That means your younger brother was also

---

* The Mun Se-gwang Incident was an assassination attempt on Park Chung-
  hee by Mun Se-gwang, a North Korean resident of Japan, on August 15,
  1974. Park survived, but his wife and a high school student were killed.
  Mun later confessed that he had been aided by the General Association
  of Korean Residents in Japan (Chongryon), leading to increased tensions
  between Japan, North Korea, and South Korea. [Translator]

All the Way to Tsushima

looking at us from over there today," I said, stumbling a little on my way down the hill. Chŏng Chŏng-mun walked along behind us, not saying a word.

"Some people might call this childish sentimentalism, and maybe it is, but you can see Tsushima even more clearly from Pusan. I used to see it all the time."

"What's so sentimental about that? If anything, I wish it were sentimental, but it's not, which is precisely the problem."

We headed down the steep slope and got into the car, which we'd parked on the side of the mountain. Still saying nothing, Chŏng Chŏng-mun slowly stepped on the gas and started driving.

When we'd driven halfway down the mountain, he suddenly stopped the car and flung his face down on the steering wheel, bursting into tears.

"What the hell are we doing here?" Chŏng Chŏng-mun said in a strained voice as the tears rolled down his face. Sitting in the backseat, Ri Sin-ki and I didn't know where to look with our own tear-filled eyes, so we turned away from each other and looked out the window.

Chŏng Chŏng-mun continued to cry like that for some time, his graying hair and his shoulders trembling, but eventually he pulled himself together and started driving again. After a while, he called out my name in a soft voice.

"Kim-*san*," he said, addressing me formally by my last name. "What on earth is a 'nation' or a 'race,' anyway?"

"How the hell should I know?" I replied angrily. "All I know is that you burst into tears just now."

For some reason, I couldn't help but getting intensely angry. I felt the urge to scream at something, but I didn't know what—or where—to scream.

One's Place

(*Ichi*, 1940)

Early one cold, dreary morning in Akihabara, after watching an all-night dress rehearsal at a theater in Tsukiji, I was walking down a long flight of stairs on my way to go help Tanaami move out of his place in Okachimachi.

Halfway down the stairs, I stopped on the landing and saw Tanaami walking up, wearing his school uniform. When he saw me, he came running up the stairs.

"I thought I told you to wait for me. Didn't you get the letter I sent by express mail yesterday . . . ?" I said, waiting for Tanaami to catch his breath beside me.

"Yeah, I got it, I got it. But I have to go in to work today. Sorry for the short notice, but I left a letter on my desk. My stuff's all packed up. Would you mind taking care of it for me?"

"I see . . . . Do you know of any movers? I haven't hired one yet."

"Oh, okay, I'll ask the movers my company uses. Once I get to the office, I'll send them over, so just get everything ready and wait for them. Thanks, man," he said, raising his hand in gratitude as he dashed up the stairs.

"You're wearing your school uniform to work?"

"Yep," he said, looking back at me for a second before disappearing into the train station.

Tanaami had said he attended evening classes in the law department at the same school as me. I got to know him when he joined our school's literary journal, which was like an alumni magazine, after we tried to recruit more members from the night school students. We decided to rent an apartment together and start cooking for ourselves after I went over to his place for the third time. He'd bought a big bottle of sake that we finished off with my friend Iwamoto, who had come with me that night. When we decided to live together, he slapped me hard on the shoulder and said, "Hey, Ōsawa! Don't think about it too much, okay? It's no big deal to me."

At first, I didn't understand what he was talking about. But after he said it three or four more times, I got the message.

When I happened to publish an essay in the official magazine of a certain organization, I used the penname Ōsawa Teruo, borrowing it from the name of a character in a friend's novel. Ever since then, my friends had called me by my penname—not my real name, Chang Ŭng-sŏ— as though they had an unspoken pact.

What Tanaami meant was: don't worry about being Korean. Of course, he probably said it out of goodwill, but at that moment, it made me even more self-conscious.

I'd been born and educated in Japan, so I knew almost no Korean and even less about Korean customs. Perhaps for that reason, all of my friends at school were Japanese, and in my interactions with them, they never made me feel like a Korean or anything like that. At any rate, Tanaami was no doubt just trying to be friendly.

He said it was lonely living alone, so he'd started frequenting cafes and getting behind in his studies. Plus, he said, it wasn't very healthy to eat out all the time. By contrast, I was sick of having to share a room with three other people in a house in Ōimachi owned by a Korean guy named Kang.

So Tanaami and I spent a day walking around

Komagome looking for apartment houses with rooms for rent, but we couldn't find any that day. After pledging to keep working at it, we went our separate ways. At school the next day, when I told my friend Waizumi that I was looking for a room, he said there might be one in his apartment house in Tabata and suggested I stop by with him that evening on our way to watch the dress rehearsal in Tsukiji. We went over together after school. As luck would have it, there was a room available, so I signed the rental agreement and sent a letter to Tanaami by express mail telling him to skip work the next day and wait for me to come over to help him move.

When I went up to Tanaami's room, I found two wicker trunks sitting on his desk and his bedding rolled up on the floor in the middle of the room. Someone had slipped a piece of paper under the rope tied around the trunks. I sat down on the bedding and took the paper out. It said:

> Sorry, but something came up. Could you move my stuff by yourself? And I haven't paid last month's rent. Sorry, but could you pay it for me before you leave? It's ten yen.

THE TRIAL OF PAK TAL AND OTHER STORIES

I crumpled up the note and threw it away.

Before long, the owner of the house came up the stairs, asking who was there. Since it was still the beginning of the month, I hadn't touched my allowance of seventy yen, so I paid the ten yen from that.

As I sat on the bedding, the fatigue from staying up all night suddenly hit me. I rested my head on the trunks and was just starting to nod off when the movers arrived.

After moving Tanaami's stuff, I moved my things from Ōimachi.

When I finally put our desks and bookcases in their respective places, the four-and-a-half-mat room was almost full. I had a lot of books. Tanaami only had five or six novels, so they all fit on top of his desk. There was a small, shallow alcove that was the perfect size for my bookshelf. I lined up our desks on either side of the alcove. I wanted to sit next to the window, but Tanaami wasn't there to choose for himself, so I let him have that spot out of courtesy.

I'd never rented an apartment before, so I was surprised to find that it came with a concrete entryway, a closet, and a kitchen, each about the size of half a tatami mat. I went into the tiny, square kitchen, which was barely big enough to fit into. As I was washing my hands, the lady who managed the apartment house came upstairs to say hello and to tell me that I had a telephone call. I was a bit embarrassed to be receiving calls so soon after moving in. I didn't want her to think that I couldn't survive in a house without a telephone. The smirk on her freckled face seemed to say as much.

When I picked up the receiver at the counter of the office downstairs, I heard Tanaami's voice on the other end. He asked me to come get him at Tabata Station because he didn't know the way to the apartment. I'd drawn him a detailed map with directions in the letter I sent by express mail the previous day, so I was a little annoyed. I told him it was a straight shot from the station, but he insisted I come, claiming it was too much trouble to figure out by himself. Out of respect for the people in the office, I hung up the phone and went out to meet Tanaami.

In front of the station, a man in livery was selling potted flowers from the back of a truck. As women walked by, carrying their bags under their arms, they stopped to pick up the flowers, trying to decide which

THE TRIAL OF PAK TAL AND OTHER STORIES

one to buy. Tanaami was leaning against a telephone pole about ten feet away, holding one of the potted flowers and staring at the flower vender.

When he noticed me heading toward him, he laughed as he handed me the potted flower.

"Hey sorry, man. I bought this for you. It was cheap— only twenty *sen*."

"Come on, let's go. We have to buy a lot of cooking utensils, and we still have to unpack."

When we got to the front of the apartment, I pointed out our room to him and said, "I'll go put this down and grab some money. I heard there's a hardware store and a china shop at the end of this street, so go pick up some basic necessities."

"Okay, sounds good. I'll try not to break the bank," he said and headed down the narrow street in front of the apartment, his school uniform blending into the throngs of housewives out doing their shopping.

We bought a bunch of things, from pots and pans to various kitchen and pantry essentials. The total came to a little over ten yen. I immediately ordered a big bag of rice from the rice shop across the street and cooked a pot for dinner.

"I'll pick up some green onions, miso, and other stuff on my way home from work. Ōsawa, you don't have much experience cooking for yourself, do you? I can tell just by looking at you," Tanaami said while I was working in the kitchen and he was reading the evening paper, which had been delivered before we even realized it. Perhaps the delivery boy thought the previous occupant still lived here.

"I know how to cook rice, but I haven't really bought stuff like that before. Thanks, man."

"Yeah, sure," he said, apparently engrossed in the paper. Then he suddenly looked up and said, "Ōsawa! Now that we're living together, we shouldn't hide anything from each other, right?"

His eyes returned to the paper.

"Yeah, I suppose so. Although I don't really have any secrets to confess to you," I said as I brought over the pot of cooked rice and set it down on the tatami.

"Well, I do. I'll tell you when we go to bed. A bedtime story, if you will. Hahaha," he laughed, looking up at me.

"I see. Well, I look forward to it."

The rice was delicious, as home-cooked rice always is. Tanaami ate a fair amount as well. I had cooked two heaping cups of rice, but it was barely enough for the two of us.

After dinner, while Tanaami was cleaning up, I went downstairs to Apt. 8, Waizumi's room, for a smoke.

Waizumi was asleep.

"I came as soon as I could. We just finished moving in."

"Oh, hey. You're here already. Sorry I couldn't help you move. I was so tired from pulling that all-nighter last night. I don't know how you're still awake," he said, sitting halfway up on his quilt.

"Don't get up. Thanks for helping me rent the room. And sorry if I cause you any trouble from now on," I said, bowing my head as I sat down.

We'd gotten to know each other recently through a study group and other activities. He gambled a lot, so he didn't come to school very often. As a result, he kept failing his exams. Recently, though, he'd broken up with a girl he used to live with, or something like that, so he was attending classes two or three times a week.

"No, I'm the one who should thank you . . . . I heard you have a roommate . . . ."

"Yeah, he's a friend of mine named Tanaami," I replied, but I felt as if I'd forgotten to say something.

From the tone of his voice, I felt the need to explain that Tanaami was Japanese. He also seemed to be expecting that from my reply. We were silent, both of us afraid that our suspicions might be right. Still, it would have been awkward at that point to say that I'd failed to mention Tanaami was Japanese.

But Waizumi beat me to it.

"So, what's his deal? Is he also, you know, from Korea?" he said, vigorously kicking off his quilt and standing up.

"No, he's Japanese. From Gunma Prefecture, of all places," I said with a laugh as I shuffled over to the desk on my knees.

Although I couldn't see it, I sensed relief on Waizumi's face.

"That's good, cause Koreans can be pretty noisy when they get together, you know. I had no idea you were Korean—you speak better Japanese than I do."

"Oh yeah?"

I gave an artificially cheerful laugh, as if to stifle a certain kind of loneliness that began to well up within my heart.

Waizumi had gone into the kitchen and was washing his face.

"I have some hot water on the stove. Wanna come over?"

"Thanks, I'll come with you. It's tough being a bachelor again."

"You must be lonely."

There was a mirror stand on the cupboard strewn with empty bottles of ointment and other things that his girlfriend had apparently left behind.

"She'll be back before long, though," he said, rubbing his head as he came out of the kitchen.

When I returned to my room with Waizumi, Tanaami was wiping his desk with a rag. The potted flower sat neatly on the corner of the desk. I introduced the two of them.

"My name's Tanaami Kisaku. I'm from Gunma Prefecture."

"Hi, I'm Waizumi," he said, standing there looking around the room. Tanaami sat on the tatami, staring up at his face.

"Come on, sit down," I said.

"Okay," Waizumi said, leaning against the desk. I offered him some tea. After a few sips, he stood up.

"I'll be in Ōishi's room next door. I introduced you

297

One's Place

two last night. Come over and hang out with us," he said and walked out.

"What a pompous ass," Tanaami said, turning around after watching Waizumi leave.

"Don't worry, you'll warm up to him before long."

"What makes him so special? Isn't he just a student, like us?" Tanaami said, a little riled up.

"Yeah, he's a student, but he goes to a school of 'higher' learning, if you know what I mean," I laughed dryly.

"I have no idea what you're talking about, man. Who the hell is he?" Tanaami said, turning away. I looked back at him when he called me "man."

"Just wait, you'll see. Hey, why don't we discuss how to handle our living expenses?"

"Oh, did you pay my rent? How much were the movers?" he asked matter-of-factly.

"The movers were twelve yen. I paid the rent. I'll make a ledger for us to write down how much we spend per day. Then we can settle accounts at the end of the month. Let's be upfront about money with each other. To avoid any misunderstandings. Make sure you write down everything you spend, even one *sen*."

I took out an old notebook.

Tanaami, nodding his head, wrote lines in the notebook and filled in our names and the date. Under his name, he wrote, "Twenty *sen*," the amount he paid for the potted flower. I picked up a pen and calculated how much money I'd spent, planning to write the amount below my name.

"Ōsawa, you spent ten yen on the rent, twelve yen on the movers, and ten yen and eighteen *sen* on the kitchen stuff . . . . That makes thirty-two yen and eighteen *sen* total," Tanaami said.

"Yeah, plus twenty yen for the rent here . . . ."

I didn't know what to do about the ten yen for his portion of the rent, but I figured he would notice it sooner or later and say something about it, so I entered the amount he said.

"Anyway, you're the one doing all the cooking, so I don't have much to write down. Hahaha," Tanaami said, peering over my shoulder at the ledger.

I smiled at him and stood up.

"Come on, let's go to Ōishi's room next door. He graduated from the law department at our school."

"No way! The law department? How old is he?"

"Around thirty, I guess. Aren't you also in the law

department?"

"Yeah, but I'm a night student, so he probably wouldn't recognize me . . . ."

When I knocked on Ōishi's door and opened it, Waizumi was sprawled out on the floor near the entrance. Ōishi was sitting in front of two bookshelves packed with books, his nose buried in a newspaper.

"We just moved in today. Nice to be neighbors with you," I said as a formality and sat down.

"Thanks, same here," Ōishi said as he stood up and took out two floor cushions from the closet.

"Hey, introduce me," Tanaami said, jabbing me from behind.

"Ōishi, this is Tanaami. We'll be living together."

"Hello, I'm Tanaami Kisaku. I'm a direct descendant of Takenaka Hanbei."

Tanaami put both hands on the floor and bowed his head.

"Nice to meet you, I'm Ōishi. Are you in the law department?" he asked, seeing the badge on Tanaami's collar.

"Yes, I am. I hear you graduated from the same department, so I'd be grateful for any advice you might have in that regard . . . ." Tanaami said, rubbing his hands together.

Waizumi remained stretched out on the floor with a smirk on his face. When Tanaami met Waizumi earlier, he mentioned his birthplace, and now he bragged about his bloodline to Ōishi. Both comments felt unnatural to me. But then I quickly realized that he'd said those things to prove that he was Japanese.

They talked about school-related stuff, but they stuck to conventional topics, probably because it was their first time meeting each other. After drinking some tea that Ōishi brewed for us, we came out into the hallway, leaving Waizumi in the room.

"Wanna go for a drink? There are some interesting-looking places around here," Tanaami said after he closed Ōishi's door.

"I wanna get to bed early tonight. I pulled an all-nighter last night, you know. Let's do it another time, okay?"

"I see. What the hell were you doing last night anyway?"

"I was observing a dress rehearsal. For a study group."

I opened the window to let in some fresh air and took

out our quilts from the closet.

When I took out the quilts, they nearly filled up the room. Tanaami only had two quilts—a top and a bottom one—and a thin quilt with sleeves.

"Ōsawa, you have four quilts? Gimme one of those. A sleeping pad is fine. This room looks like it gets cold at night."

"You'll probably get cold if that's all you have. Here, I'll lay one quilt down for you, so use it as a sleeping pad if you want."

"Thanks. My parents said they'd send me more quilts from home, but I told them not to because my previous place was relatively warm."

"Okay, how should we lay these out? Ah, I have an idea: why don't you sleep near the kitchen, since you'll be getting up before me in the morning to cook the rice?" I said, grabbing a quilt.

He fell silent for a while, apparently lost in thought, and then replied, "Umm, I don't like sleeping by the door. Let's put our heads toward the window."

"Okay, then I'll sleep there."

I put my quilt down with my head toward the kitchen and my feet toward the door.

When I crawled under the covers, a wave of fatigue washed over me. Tanaami was spreading out a bedsheet on top of the sleeping pad. The sheet was made up of hand towels that had been stitched together.

"Shall I tell you my secret now?" he said, taking off his clothes.

"Sure, let's hear it."

"Lemme turn off the lights first."

Tanaami turned off the lights and got into bed, scratching the area around his waist. Turning over onto his stomach, he lit a cigarette. The light from the street streamed in through the window above his head, projecting the windowpanes onto the opposite wall. A thin tendril of smoke drifted up from his cigarette.

"The thing is, Ōsawa . . ." he began slowly. Then he stubbed out his cigarette and rolled over onto his back before blurting out, "I haven't been going to the university."

I was a bit surprised, but I played it cool.

"Oh, so you were lying about being in the law department?"

"We live together, so you would've found out sooner or later. I'll tell you what's really going on, but please don't tell anybody else."

"Why would I tell anybody something like that?"

"Out of respect for my father, I told him I was studying in the law department because I couldn't get into the literature department, but those were both lies," he said. He fidgeted under the covers for a while before continuing. "Actually, I have a friend in the law department. I wanted to follow him around and see what a university is really like, so I went with him to school one day. It was boring as hell, but still I thought: if I was going to graduate from middle school, I might as well enter a vocational department, but they said I couldn't because I only graduated from higher elementary school."

I was watching the shadows flicker on the wall. He glanced at my face from time to time as he spoke.

"That's when I saw that recruitment ad for the literary magazine. You know, the one you wrote," he laughed, raising his head and looking at me. I smiled back at him with the side of my face.

"I thought you had to be a student to become a member of that magazine. You know what I'm talking about, Ōsawa, but those other guys think you can't understand literature unless you go to a university.

What difference does it make whether or not you go to a university? What a bunch of fucking idiots. Of course, I don't mean you, Ōsawa . . . . So that's why I bought a uniform. I've been wearing it ever since because I paid all that money for it and because it's easier than deciding what to wear every day."

"I see . . . . That's it? That was your big secret?" I said lightheartedly.

"Yeah, that's it. Don't tell the other guys, okay? To become a writer, it doesn't matter whether or not you go to a university, right?" he asked insistently.

"No, of course not."

"I've been studying fiction for a while now, you know. Since I was sixteen. And I wrote tons of *tanka* poems when I was an apprentice at a liquor shop."

"A liquor shop? You apprenticed at a liquor shop?"

"Yeah, despite appearances, I wasn't raised with a silver spoon in my mouth like you, Ōsawa. I had to work as an errand boy for a liquor shop, so I've learned more from real life than those guys who've just been going to school all the time. Didn't someone once say that art is the product of experience?"

He was speaking more excitedly now. I couldn't get

a clear sense of what he meant by words like "art" and "literature." I had a bad feeling about him.

"Sure, you won't learn anything if you just go to school all the time," I said.

"I knew you'd understand, Ōsawa, so that's why I'm telling you all this. Don't tell the other guys, though, okay?" he said, reminding me for the umpteenth time.

"Don't worry, your secret's safe with me," I replied casually, but his secret strangely began to consume my thoughts afterward. He lay still, staring at the ceiling. I started to wonder how much longer I could go on living with him like this.

Actually, this feeling got stronger with each passing day.

He often wrote works of fiction. And he often showed them to me. They were almost entirely fantasies about a rich young man falling in love with a barmaid or a factory girl.

At first, I was more interested in the way he wrote than what he wrote. Our desks were right next to each other, so I couldn't help seeing him even when I tried not to. He'd spread out some manuscript paper and write furiously without stopping. Then, as if something had popped into his mind, he'd put down his pen and stare off into space. It was as though he were trying to summon the muses. When he noticed me glancing at him from time to time, he'd repeat the same actions over and over again. At first, I just laughed to myself and pretended not to notice, but the more he did this, the more it started to disgust me.

This happened all the time, not just when he was writing a manuscript. He would act as if he were observing something for the sake of being observed.

Even when we were strolling through the stalls at a night market, he would sometimes stand still, as though hit by an electrical shock, and focus his eyes on a point in the distance. When that happened, I refused to wait for him and just walked on ahead. Then he'd chase after me, saying, "Ōsawa, you're not a true artist."

That month, I'd written to my parents back home, asking them to send me an extra twenty yen or so. Still, I had to sell two or three books to the used bookstore in front of our apartment just to make ends meet. That was the first time I'd sold any of my books. Half the time, when Tanaami would say to me, "Come on, just let me have one drink," I'd have to go out with him simply because I had more money than he did.

One's Place

It was Saturday, the "day before payday," as Tanaami liked to say. I had a study group gathering that day in preparation for a roundtable we were holding the following day with a certain leading figure, so I came home around eight, after we'd finished.

Tanaami wasn't home yet. I'd grabbed dinner on the way home, but I wasn't sure if he'd eaten yet, so I cooked some rice. As always, I spread out a newspaper in the middle of the room and laid out some food for him so he could eat as soon as he got home. I sat at my desk drinking a cup of tea.

Tanaami finally came home around ten.

After opening the door and poking his head in, he gave me the same greeting he always did when he came home and saw me turn around.

"Sorry, man."

I could tell from his droopy eyes that he'd been drinking.

"Welcome home," I said and turned back to my desk.

Still wearing his overcoat, he moved the food on the newspaper out of the way and fell onto the floor with his head in his hands. I could hear him let out a big sigh. I continued to read my book in silence. Eventually, I could hear the sound of sniffling. He was curled up into a ball, shedding tears.

"What's wrong?" I asked, even though I suspected it was the same old thing. He turned his face away from me.

"Did something happen to you?"

Realizing I may have been wrong about the situation, I tried to speak more tenderly. His shoulders began to shake violently. I closed my book and turned around.

"Ōsawa, can I tell you something?"

When he lifted up his face, it was wet with tears and flushed from drinking. His voice was oddly plaintive.

"Sure, what is it?"

"I got my paycheck today, actually. Tomorrow is Sunday, so they moved it up a day. Anyway . . . you might call this crazy, but do you remember that letter that arrived the other day from a girl named Akemi? Well, I wanted to go see her, so I went over to Takarabune, the bar in Ueno where she works, but I couldn't bring myself to go in. I don't know why. So, I went to a beer hall and had a few beers before going back again, but I still couldn't go through with it. I went back and forth four different times. The problem is, she treats me like a younger brother. Two days ago, I wrote to her saying I want to be more than just brother and sister. You know what I mean, right? She treats me like a younger brother, man. Do you know how that makes me feel? Do you, Ōsawa?"

He was facing me as he spoke, but he gradually shifted his gaze to the wall, where he stared at a single point as he finished his story. I wanted to say something snide like, "No, not really. Is that all that happened?" My eyes returned to my desk for a moment, but I sat quietly facing him.

"The next time I see her, I'll know her true feelings for me because of the letter I sent two days ago. Dammit! I'm such a coward!" he said with more than a touch of theatricality. Then he took off the hat he was wearing and slammed it down on the potted flower on his desk. I don't know what it was called, but the tall flower broke apart under the weight of his hat.

He was no longer crying, but his face—with those long sideburns of his—had an ugly glow to it.

"Would you like me to go with you? It's a bit late to go tonight, though," I said noncommittally, looking at the clock.

"Really? Thanks, man," he said, already getting to his feet. I got a little flustered. He cleaned up the scattered

THE TRIAL OF PAK TAL AND OTHER STORIES

flower petals and put on his hat.

"Isn't it too late?"

The clock showed 10:50.

"No, we still have over an hour. We can make it."

He walked toward the door.

I was sleepy, but I was the one who had brought it up, so I had no choice but to go with him.

When we boarded the streetcar and bought our tickets, he said, "Of course, let's split the bill between us." He was in high spirits again.

I was uncomfortable with him thinking I'd fallen into his trap, but I was also curious to see for myself what kind of woman this Akemi really was.

The streets were much quieter after ten o'clock. The streetcar screeched and shook like mad as it sped down the street. By the time we passed Shinobazu Pond in Ueno, it was so dark and deserted that it felt as if we were passing through the mountains.

I thought Takarabune was an ordinary café, but it was a hostess bar. Tanaami pretended to ignore the women who greeted us as we walked in. When he spotted an empty table in the back, he looked down and walked straight toward it. I followed him, sensing everyone's eyes on me.

One's Place

Tanaami puffed on a cigarette, watching the smoke rise. I looked around the inside of the bar. Red tables and deep booths were lined up right next to each other. As far as I could tell, there seemed to be twenty women standing around, all of them wearing the same gaudy kimonos. I was surprised that a guy like Tanaami would frequent a place like this by himself. I could never do something like that.

A thin woman wearing a kimono with a more subdued pattern than the others came over to our table. When she came up beside Tanaami, she plopped herself down next to him and squealed, "Why, it's my little boy Kii! You finally came. Where have you been?"

She raised his chin with her slender fingers and pretended to kiss him. When she saw me, she shrugged her shoulders and giggled.

Despite her affections, Tanaami remained completely still, his eyes glued to a spot he'd been staring at for a while. The woman put her arm around his shoulders and hugged him. Then she tilted her head a little and peered into his face.

I looked away. In a booth under a potted palm near the center of the room, a portly middle-aged man was sticking out his round, wide belly. The women sitting and standing around him were cackling with laughter as they slapped his belly and took turns sticking their fingers into his belly button.

"Shall I bring you a drink?" the woman asked when I turned around, her face nuzzled against Tanaami's shoulder.

I was at a loss for words, so Tanaami finally turned to her and said, "Bring us some beers."

"Hold on a sec, okay?"

She stood up, placing both hands on Tanaami's shoulders, and walked away toward the back.

Tanaami took out another cigarette and tapped it on the table, leaning his head to one side.

"Hey, man, I'm really sorry."

"What for? So . . . was that woman Akemi?"

"Yeah, that's her. Whaddya think? She looks older, but she's only twenty-three."

"Yeah, that must put her at a real disadvantage," I replied as I spotted her coming back with the beers on a tray and a smile on her face. She was probably lying about her age. She looked at least twenty-seven or twenty-eight. It seemed like she was wearing a plain kimono to make herself look even younger. Her face was slim, with a broad forehead and prominent cheekbones. She was wearing thick pink lipstick, but it overpowered her narrow face, making her look rather unattractive. She didn't look like a café waitress at all. She looked more like a housewife with kids who was doing some work on the side.

She made an interesting contrast to the fat woman wearing heavy makeup who had come back with her when she brought the beers and was now sitting next to me with nothing to do.

After two or three more beers, the two women were chattering away amongst themselves when a loud, shrill bell suddenly rang. "Ah, it's closing time," the woman next to me exclaimed, stretching her arms as she stood up to leave.

Tanaami and Akemi were whispering about something or other. I could hear her saying something about going to see a movie tomorrow because she was working the late shift. Once the bell rang, the other women quieted down and gradually began to disperse.

"Okay, I got it. Just gimme the bill," Tanaami said, preparing to leave. She whined in disapproval, looking up at his face and tugging at his sleeve. He started to sit down again. But then she got up. Tanaami seemed a little confused. I chuckled to myself.

"How much is it?" Tanaami asked, a little upset. Still looking up at his face with a seductive smile, she pulled out the check from her waistband and slid it across the table. Tanaami took it and turned it over.

"Twelve yen. Okay, here you go," he said, pulling out his pay envelope from his inside pocket. He quickly hid it by his side and threw down two ten-yen bills.

She came back with the change, but instead of putting it in Tanaami's hand right away, she continued flirting with him, whispering into his ear and slapping him on the shoulder. I waited for him at the exit.

We decided to get off the streetcar one stop early and walk the rest of the way back to the apartment. I felt sick, probably from drinking too much beer. As we walked along in silence, the sounds of our shoes echoed loudly through the hushed dark streets.

"I heard you talking about going to the movies or something . . . ." I said.

"I don't know what to do. She wants to go tomorrow, hahaha. She thinks I go to school during the day," he said, quickening his pace to catch up with me.

One's Place

You don't go at night either, I thought, but I said, "That's a tough one. You can't take the day off from work, can you?"

"No, not really . . . . but I have an idea that might work," he said, changing into his slippers at the entrance to our apartment house. He pointed toward the window of the management office. "Can you call me tomorrow? At my office. Tell them a telegram arrived from my hometown saying my aunt died."

"A telegram? What time should I call?"

"We promised to meet in front of Kaminarimon Gate in Asakusa at noon, so ten should be fine. Don't worry about it, I told my company my aunt got sick the other day."

"Okay. I'll give you a call around ten, so make sure you're there."

I laid down our quilts.

Even as he took off his clothes, he was giddy with excitement.

The next day, I went into a phone booth and placed a call to Tanaami.

"What?! My aunt died?! A telegram came?!"

As I listened to him through the receiver, I could

imagine him on the other end, expressing his shock and dismay.

That day, Tanaami didn't come home until after midnight.

He opened the door quietly, but when he realized I was still awake, he came in with his usual arrogant excuse: "Sorry, man."

He was breathing heavily, and I could smell the alcohol on his breath.

He received a monthly salary of fifty-five yen, of which he sent home ten or fifteen yen a month.

The letters he got from home were stamped with the words "Tanaami Rubber Tire Repair" on the back. According to him, his family was now making a meager living off an old tire repair shop, which they'd acquired after their business failed. He often talked about his father's business failure. Even with his other friends, he used the term "business failure" particularly often.

When he had trouble falling asleep right away, even after we turned off the lights, he'd talk a lot about his family. I decided not to say a word about mine, though.

"What kind of business was it—the one he started with 50,000 yen?"

One's Place

"You know the rubber soles on Japanese sandals? They're made from old tires . . . . That was his business."

"Wow, if he sank 50,000 yen into it, it must have been a pretty big operation."

"Yeah, it failed, but I'm really proud of my father. At first, the soles were mostly made by Sanka people. My father noticed they were hard workers. That's why he hired so many of them to work at his factory."

"Did you say 'Sanka'? Aren't they those mountain people who've been seen as different than the true Yamato people of Japan? I heard about them once . . . ."

"That's right. I think my father's greatness was seeing something in them. If you put them to work with ordinary Japanese people, they get into fights all the time. One time, they got into a pretty big argument inside the factory. My father assembled all the factory workers in the yard. Then he said something interesting to them. He asked one of the regular Japanese guys: how do you guys take a shit? The guy came forward and pretended to squat on the ground. Then he asked one of the Sanka guys: how do you take a shit? He did the same thing. The next thing you know, my father shouted at them: See, you guys are all the same human beings. I really admired my father at that moment. He thought of things no one else would ever think of."

Sometimes he'd even talk about how many artistic geniuses there were in his family, like his father being a famous Nagauta singer or his younger sister being a classical dance prodigy at the age of thirteen. I'd listen to him with my eyes half open as I nodded off. Before I knew it, I'd fall asleep without even hearing him finish.

In the mornings, he'd cook the rice and eat breakfast before leaving for work. I'd get up and eat later, but I slept by the kitchen, so he'd often pass by my pillow. To open the kitchen door, you had to lift it up with some force because the quilt often got stuck on it. Even so, all he had to do was fold up his own quilt and pull mine over, but maybe that was too much trouble for him because as soon as he got up, he'd stand directly over my face and open the door. When I was asleep, I didn't notice, but when I was awake, I'd shut my eyes because bits of dirt seemed to fall from his crotch. I should have asked him to change places with me, but he said he hated sleeping by the door, so that wouldn't work.

Furthermore, I was often awoken by the sound of him brushing his teeth or gargling. He had two small hand mirrors. He brought one of them into the kitchen to see the inside of his mouth as he brushed his teeth repeatedly until he was satisfied that they were clean. When he finally finished brushing, he'd sit cross-legged on his quilt, which was still lying on the floor. It was now time to take care of his hair and his face. He'd try parting his hair many different ways. When he finally settled on a 7:3 side part, he'd align the mirrors so he could see the front and back of his head. Once he saw that the back was combed, he'd comb the front. He'd try things like combing his hair backwards, pinching his nose, and then rolling his eyes around. On mornings when I was in a good mood, I'd bury my face in my quilt and try to resist the urge to laugh. Sometimes, though, I burst out laughing, which took him by surprise.

After one or two months of this, we started to get tired of each other. He appeared to expect something of me that I never managed to fulfill. Plus, I started to get sick of the way he insisted on his superiority in various situations. I don't know where that feeling of superiority came from.

My semester exams were scheduled to end on March 10. I was planning to spend the upcoming semester break at my cousin's place in Yokosuka.

I told Tanaami on his way out in the morning that I was leaving that evening as soon as my classes ended. But when I rushed home from school, the lady from the management office grabbed me and said that Tanaami had called a little earlier asking me not to leave for Yokosuka until he got back because he had something he needed to talk about. To tide me over for almost a month in Yokosuka, I packed up some books and personal belongings. Then I cooked some rice, thinking I'd wait to eat dinner with Tanaami.

He came home around seven, much later than his usual time of five-thirty.

"Hey sorry, man," he said, flinging his hat on his desk and flopping down on the floor. He'd been drinking. I tore myself away from my desk and dug into the food I'd left out on the newspaper.

"You're a little late today. I heard you called saying you wanted to talk to me about something, so I was waiting for you."

"I know, I know . . . but what's the hurry? Let's eat first," he said, taking a heaping bowl of rice from me and shoveling the grains into his mouth.

"I still have enough time to get there tonight, but when someone says they have something to talk to you about, you don't want to be kept waiting."

I remembered how he'd just nodded as he headed out that morning when I told him I was going to Yokosuka.

"Well, it's not that big a deal. I just didn't have time to tell you when I left this morning. I'll tell you in a sec."

We fell silent for a while as we finished eating.

Tanaami washed the dishes in the kitchen. I lit a cigarette and glanced at the evening paper.

After noisily stacking the dishes, Tanaami came out wiping his hands with a dishcloth. When he was done, he chucked it into the kitchen and slammed the door shut with his foot. I pushed the newspaper and the box of cigarettes toward him.

"Hurry up and tell me, it's getting late," I said, looking up at the clock to give him a hint.

He lit a match and covered it with both hands as he twisted his face to light a cigarette.

"Okay. Actually, it's about money," he blurted out, looking back at my face.

"What do you mean?"

"Can't you see I'm broke, you idiot?" he said, sounding

annoyed.

"I had no idea. It's still the beginning of the month. I thought you still had some money from your last paycheck."

"You gotta be kidding me," he scoffed. He got up and went over to the window.

"Come on, sit down. If you don't have any money, we gotta figure something out. I'll be at my cousin's house for the rest of the month, so I told my parents not to send me my allowance this month. Actually, I was supposed to go back home, but as you know my family's not very well-off, so I couldn't afford to."

"You probably thought I'd steal it, didn't you?" he said, flinging the cigarette butt toward the street.

"No, that's not what I meant at all."

"Whatever, it doesn't matter," he said, gazing down at the street for a while. He sat on the windowsill and folded his hands together on his knees. He stared at me, nodding his head slowly up and down. I avoided his gaze and looked at the illustrations in the newspaper on the floor.

"You want me to move out, don't ya?" he said, breaking the silence. His tone of voice was different.

I didn't know how to reply. To be honest, I was a little

shell-shocked from what he'd said.

"If you want me to move out, just tell me. One of my friends has been begging me to move in with him since last month. But I've been putting up with it like this. Do you know how that makes me feel? Do ya?"

"What do you have to put up with? If you're tired of living together, why don't you just say so?"

"Jeez, you really are fucking clueless," he said, turning away in a huff.

"What the hell's that supposed to mean?"

I was starting to get a little angry as well.

He turned around and recrossed his arms over his chest.

"Fine! If you can't say it, then I will. Have you ever once thought about the fact that you're Korean?" he spat out.

I felt myself go weak at the knees. I frantically looked at the floor. My chest began to tighten.

"What do you think the apartment lady said to me when we first moved in? She grabbed me and called me a Korean. Even that weird friend of yours Waizumi said the same damn thing: 'I thought you were Korean at first.' And it's not just them, either. All your fuckin' friends who come over think I'm Korean, don't they?"

I hung my head lower and lower. Tears filled my eyes. I was unable to move. He went on, getting more and more worked up.

"Even my old man has been telling me to hurry up and leave for a while now. He says I shouldn't live with Koreans because you never know what they're gonna do next. But I felt sorry for you, so I stayed. And yet, after all I've done for you, you make a fuss over a measly ten or twenty yen . . . . I thought you might be a little more understanding since you said you were a college student, but this is completely ridiculous . . . ."

He hurled an endless stream of abuse at my face. I tried my best not to let him see my big messy tears fall onto the tatami. As I sat there, I felt my body begin to shrink.

Apparently, he was still talking, but I could no longer hear what he was saying. I quickly pulled out my coin purse and placed it on the tatami in front of him.

"Here's some money. Move your things out while I'm gone," I said at last.

Then I rushed out the door.

Memories of My Grandmother

(Sobo no omoide, 1944/1946)

I often think of home.

And every time I remember my grandmother, I can't help but feel a pang of sadness in my heart. What a pitiful woman my grandmother was.

Our family eventually went bankrupt, so they got rid of their property and moved to Japan, but my late older brother and I were what you might call "grandma's boys," so we stayed behind with her in the village where we were born. My grandmother refused to go to Japan, insisting that she wanted to be buried in Korea. We barely got by on the allowance of fifteen or twenty yen we received from our family in Japan each month. Sooner or later, though, we'd have to join our parents in Japan, even if that meant leaving our grandmother behind.

Before long, my grandmother and I lost my middle

brother, who was the darkest and the smallest of us four siblings. Then we received a telegram from Japan saying that my father had died. My grandmother's hair seemed to turn white all at once. I remember how my grandmother's eyes—more wrinkled than before— brimmed with tears every day. Even after that, though, my grandmother continued to suffer more misfortune. After a while, my father's remains were brought home for burial at the *seonsan* (ancestral burial mound) in our hometown. His remains had been entrusted to someone else, but around the time his remains came back, my uncle—who had been working in Tokyo, like my parents—temporarily returned to his own hometown. He showed up soon after my father's funeral.

He cut an unusual figure in his Japanese livery and military-style boots, which I found strangely hard to get used to. At my mother's request, he'd come to bring me to Japan. He said he'd take me to his own house for the time being and then take me with him when he returned to Tokyo. I probably wanted to go to Japan to be with my mother, as any ten-year-old would. I don't remember it very clearly, but I left with my uncle the next day, so I must have agreed to it. My poor grandmother . . . she probably couldn't bring herself to tell him she didn't want to let me go live with my mother. She'd just lost her only son while he was still young (my father was thirty-seven when he died) and watched another grandson die right before her eyes—and now she had to endure the loneliness of living all by herself.

The day after the funeral, I departed with my uncle, carrying a cloth bundle on my back. My uncle's hometown was about twelve or thirteen *ri* (thirty miles) away. I boarded the train, looking back repeatedly at my grandmother, who had come to the station to see me off. When the train began to move, my grandmother fell to her knees where she was standing and burst into tears, beating her fists against the ground. I quickly pulled my head back inside the train and tried to somehow hide my tears from my uncle, who was sitting across from me.

That was my first trip on a train in my life. I seem to remember arriving at my uncle's house at night. The house was swarming with children, and the *ondol*-style room lined with bulrush mats was filled with the acrid smell of piss. When I bowed to introduce myself to my fat aunt, who was sitting on the floor with a kid on her lap covered in boils, she looked straight over my head

Memories of My Grandmother

and started scolding my good-for-nothing uncle. "What the hell do you think you're doing," she said, "bringing a kid this size into our house when you still don't know when you're going back to Japan? Where are we going to find enough rice to feed a kid like this, who probably eats like a horse?" I'd seen my share of misfortune when my family went bankrupt and was torn apart, but that night was the first time I had to ask other people to take care of me. Having been born and raised in a well-to-do family, which still retained some traces of its aristocratic *yangban* roots, I was mortified, and my pride was deeply wounded. As I spent the night in the corner of that room, which reeked of piss, I firmly resolved to go home to my grandmother the next day no matter what it took. Even if I had to ask people for directions, I'd find my way home one way or another . . . .

The next morning, as luck would have it, my uncle's family said they were going to the train station to pick someone up (or perhaps it was to drop someone off). They told me to come along with them, making me carry the kid covered in boils on my back. For some reason, I still remember that we went at 8 am. Maybe someone told me that the train was arriving or leaving at that time. At the station (the one I'd arrived at the previous night), I said I had to go take a piss, so I put the kid down and gave him to my aunt, giving me a chance to escape. My "plan," as I recall, was to follow the train tracks back the way I'd come until I reached a place I recognized.

I walked. I never got hungry. All I could think about was how much I missed my grandmother. For someone like me who had never traveled very far from home, I was a little frightened by the looks I received from passersby on the street. Still, I kept walking. I was worried I might lose sight of the train tracks if I only followed the road, so I walked gingerly along the tracks, even when the construction workers yelled at me. I walked the whole day.

Finally, I realized I'd reached the entrance to Masan, which looked familiar to me. I got excited. I knew it was only about two *ri* (five miles) from Masan to the village where my house was. By the time I passed by the school my older brother had graduated from and arrived at the entrance to my village, the sun was just beginning to sink behind the mountains to the west. That's when I saw an old woman standing on the road under a row of poplar trees in the light of the setting sun. She was looking at me,

Memories of My Grandmother

shielding the sun from her eyes with her hand. She looked like my grandmother. She *was* my grandmother! I started running so fast I couldn't breathe. My grandmother started running as well, although she tripped and fell down once along the way.

"*Hal-me* (Grandma)!"

"Tal-su!"

We hugged each other there on the road. Then we cried.

My grandmother said she had a feeling I'd be coming home that day for some reason. Believing this without a shadow of a doubt, my grandmother had naturally prepared dinner for two—including me—and had come out to meet me in front of the house. I still ask myself: at that moment, why did my grandmother instinctively believe I was coming home and go out to meet me like that? I still can't fully explain this, even to myself. I also wonder: what would my grandmother have done if I hadn't come home that day? Would she have gone out every day and stood on the road like that in the evening sun, shielding her eyes with her hand as she watched for me to appear on the horizon?

About two years later, however, my older brother

came to Korea to get me, and I ended up leaving my grandmother behind after all and moving to Japan. Then I got so wrapped up in my daily life that I didn't even know she had died until it was too late. My grandmother spent the final years of her life with another aunt who had taken her in after I moved to Japan. I wonder if my grandmother waited for me a few days after I left, standing on that road under those poplar trees. Alas, I'll never know . . . .